Jews in New Mexico Since World War II

Jews in New Mexico
Since World War II

Henry J. Tobias

University of New Mexico Press | Albuquerque

First paperback printing 2024 | ISBN 978-0-8263-4419-9

Library of Congress Cataloging-in-Publication Data

Tobias, Henry Jack.
Jews in New Mexico since World War II / Henry J. Tobias.
    p. cm.
Includes index.
ISBN 978-0-8263-4418-2 (cloth : alk. paper)
1. Jews—New Mexico—History—20th century.
2. Jews—New Mexico—History—21st century.
3. New Mexico—Ethnic relations.
I. Title.
  F805.J5T63 2008
  978.9'004924—dc22

                            2007052614

Book design and type composition by Melissa Tandysh
Composed in 10.8/13 Minion Pro
Display type is Horley Old Style MT Std

Contents

	Preface	vii
	Acknowledgments	xi
CHAPTER ONE:	Historical Background	1
CHAPTER TWO:	Population Growth, 1940–2000	7
CHAPTER THREE:	Social and Economic Change	18
CHAPTER FOUR:	The Growth of Secular Organizations	36
CHAPTER FIVE:	Congregational Growth and Religious Change	61
CHAPTER SIX:	Interfaith Activity	93
CHAPTER SEVEN:	Issues	105
CHAPTER EIGHT:	The Jewish Presence	125
	Conclusions and Afterthoughts	143
	Appendix: Congregations Listed in the Link	147
	Notes	149
	Index	165

Preface

My previous volume, *A History of the Jews in New Mexico*, which appeared in 1990, ended its historical coverage roughly in 1980. No special event occurred at that time to clearly demarcate that date as the end of an era. Publication considerations as to length, ready documentation—such as the appearance of the census of 1980, the latest available at that time—and proximity to the time in which I researched and wrote dictated the arbitrary date of conclusion.

Public interest in the original work led the publisher and myself to the decision to create an updated version of the work. At first we considered the addition of a chapter to the existing book that would carry the story to the year 2000. That course soon proved inadvisable. The quantity and importance of new material could not be treated adequately in so short an addition. It also raised the dilemma of whether readers would be interested in acquiring a second edition of a work that merely added a chapter. We decided, therefore, that the new work should stand as an independent volume, albeit a short one.

Just as 1980 offered no special point in time to end the original volume, it also did not provide an adequate starting point for a new one. To understand where events stood in 1980 one had to look back to the period of World War II and its immediate aftermath. This need was true for Jews everywhere, for the Jews of New Mexico, for New Mexico itself, and, indeed, for the American nation as a whole.

For the Jews, the defining events of the war and immediate postwar years, that is, 1939 to 1948, were the Holocaust and the creation of the state of Israel. Nevertheless, subsequent to that time, much that was new and important also occurred as a process of evolution or through adaptation to new issues in American life. Nothing that happened between 1948 and 2000, however, could approach the dramatic impact of the war and the years immediately following as a starting point. In later decades the processes of change in American history, the more local issues of New Mexican history, and the internal communal developments of the Jewish population provide an avalanche of issues and materials that made carrying the narrative to the year 2000 as natural and convenient a point of division as I could devise.

When the Jewish population in New Mexico consisted of a small number of families, biography served as a major approach to description. The sources—memoirs or family recollections, a few business and institutional records, and the public activities of individuals—allowed a reasonable description to be recalled and analyzed. As Jewish numbers grew and their social organization followed suit, the use of simple statistics to describe them became a necessary addition for comprehending long-term development, although individual and family biography remained an important dimension of historical description. Unfortunately, the space available to depict them diminished as numbers grew, and the size of the projected volume failed to keep pace with those increases.

The rapid expansion of organized Jewish communal activity in New Mexico after World War II produced a plethora of new sources and a strengthened relationship with the world of larger Jewish issues. Such matters make the postwar era in New Mexico far more complex than its prewar history. And with the passage of time the pace of that complexity has continued to increase. This historian's heart gladdens at the implications of that complexity. It serves as one measure of maturity. But the expanding quantity of materials available for study also causes this historian's heart to sink at the prospect of mastering all the sources and answering the variety of questions that might be considered necessary for him to fulfill his obligations. In any case, I believe a "complete" history is a fiction. However, one hopes that the major issues crucial to the story are at least considered in a manner that suffices for the time in which this history is written. As is always the case with subject matter worthy of study, succeeding generations of historians will improve upon this historian's efforts as more information comes to light. May they enjoy the quest as much as I did.

Acknowledgments

The aid an author receives in producing a manuscript is sometimes not readily appreciated—often by those who provided assistance. As I have discovered, the closer a historical study comes to the present the more one comes to rely on persons who have lived through the era under description. The information received from them must be described as "documentary" as fully as those more usual bits of paper evidence on which the historian writing of a more distant past usually relies. Interviewing a living "document" in person or by telephone has been strange to this author who has spent most of his research life with the paper sort one does not thank in a personal way. However, I do not include in these acknowledgments those persons who have been directly involved in this history itself as sources or actors. They appear either as part of the text or in the notes where their roles are formally recognized.

My appreciation here is directed to those persons from whom I sought aid but who were not necessarily actors in the events described. Nevertheless, their knowledge was invaluable. Here I thank Maurice Rosenthal, Cliff Blaugrund, Paula Wolf, Walter

Kahn, Leah Kellogg, Iris Keltz, Irv Roth, Milton Seligman, and Judy and Peter Weinreb, who helped identify sources unknown to me or directed me to others who could. My gratitude to Susan Abonyi of the *Link* for her patience. My computer guru, Sheldon Liebman, made the appearance of the manuscript literally possible.

I also acknowledge a special debt and my gratitude to Joyce Kaser, who read all of the manuscript early and pointed out to me numerous gaps and inconsistencies my own eyes did not detect as well as bringing me closer to the reader's perspective. I also thank, with parental pride, the skilled editorial eyes of my daughter, Ruth Tobias, and of Suzanne Simons, both of whom read the manuscript and offered invaluable suggestions. To those I may have inadvertently forgotten, my deepest apologies.

CHAPTER ONE

Historical Background

$\mathcal{M}$odern Jewish settlement in New Mexico began with the American occupation and annexation in the last half of the 1840s in what is now known as the American Southwest. From that time until 1880 the Jewish arrivals were heavily Germanic (Ashkenazic) immigrants in origin and frequently related to each other—younger extended family members often following older ones to residence in the New World. Not until the census of 1880 did the first American-born adult Jewish settlers appear in New Mexico. In the decade of the 1880s, Jews existed in sufficient numbers and attained sufficient confidence to create communal institutions. The first of the social organizations, a chapter of B'nai B'rith (Sons of the Covenant), a national fraternal order to unite Jewish men to promote their highest interests and those of humanity, came to life in Albuquerque. That was in 1883. A religious congregation followed in Las Vegas (Congregation Montefiore, 1884) and another in Albuquerque in 1897 (Congregation Albert). In the early 1920s, Albuquerque acquired a second congregation, B'nai Israel, to accommodate the desire for a more traditional religious expression among New Mexico's Jewry. In the mid-1930s Santa Fe's Jews formed their own chapter of B'nai B'rith. These institutions accounted for all the formal organization of New Mexico's Jews before 1940.

By and large, the pre–World War II Jewish residents made their living through engagement in business enterprises. A number of them, especially prior to the coming of the railroad in 1879–80, achieved exceptional economic success in ventures relying on retail and wholesale trade and in supplying army installations and Indian reservations in far-flung locations with goods that could not readily be brought to New Mexico by the military itself. Such trade extended from the largest towns in the territory to some of the smallest. The most prominent of these merchants—the Spiegelbergs, Seligmans, Staabs, and Ilfelds (whose enterprise continued to exist and flourish long after the others became defunct)—were among the wealthiest Anglos in New Mexico.

This "golden age" of post–Civil War economic activity came to a close with the arrival of the railroads in 1879–80. Freight cars sharply altered the existing economies. Trade based on the wagon trains of the Santa Fe Trail declined precipitously. So too did the established lending practices of the time, which had included relatively long-term credit granted by merchants in shipping and receiving goods. The time involved to settle accounts became much shorter. Many of the merchants, Jews as well as non-Jews, faced problems of adapting to the new conditions, which often proved less favorable for them than they had in the past.

The hardest hit town by the revolution in transportation was Santa Fe, the territorial capital and the largest town. Its particular disadvantage lay in the fact that the main line of the railroad by-passed the city, leaving it with a depressed economy that lasted roughly through the First World War. Until the railroad came, the city had contained the largest number of Jews of any town in New Mexico. With the advent of the railroad, Las Vegas assumed first place.

The city of Albuquerque, and for a time Las Vegas, acquired the major immediate economic benefits of the railroad's appearance. Growth in Jewish numbers, as witnessed by their institutional as well as economic development, followed the growth of the towns. The Jewish population of Santa Fe, however, declined, as did that of Las Vegas several decades later when its economy encountered hard times. Albuquerque's Jewish numbers, by contrast, continued to grow.

By 1940 the Jewish population of New Mexico exceeded 1,100, its growth rate roughly keeping pace with that of the state's population. In their ethnic character, these Jews still often reflected their early Germanic background although the younger generations had assimilated heavily into Anglo culture and had acquired a sensitivity to the presence of the large Hispanic and Native American populations. Some more Eastern European immigrants from parts of Prussia, the western Russian Empire, and Austria-Hungary slowly entered the picture. However, the fact that in the 1930s only about 10 percent of Albuquerque's Jews could use Yiddish, the hallmark language of East European Jewry, reflects the American assimilation and continuing Germanic background of most of the Jewish population of New Mexico.

By the 1930s, East European Jewish immigrants to the United

States, who had begun to arrive in large numbers in the 1880s, far outweighed the earlier Germanic influx in the country at large. While before 1880 New Mexico's Jews generally resembled many other western Jewish communities in their cultural background, by 1940 the massive growth of East European Jewish numbers in the northeastern states left New Mexico's Jews of largely Germanic background a small and culturally and economically distinct community compared to the large centers of Jewish population in the Northeast. However, as noted, the Jews of New Mexico had adapted themselves well to their chosen but relatively isolated place of residence.

The economic character of the Jewish population in New Mexico did not change dramatically between 1880 and 1940. Jews remained largely entrepreneurs even though a few ventured into ranching in the latter decades of the nineteenth century. Their enterprises, however, were for the most part distinctly smaller in comparison to the earlier, prerailroad, large-scale businesses that had supplied Indian reservations and forts. Second- and third-generation Jews, with levels of education available to them undreamed of by their immigrant forefathers, slowly appeared in the ranks of professionally trained practitioners such as attorneys and medical doctors. Before 1940, however, their numbers did not significantly alter the heavy predominance of the middle-class entrepreneurs.

The small Jewish population, often fairly well educated, long played a significant role in the life of the general community. They held public office and participated in chambers of commerce and public events. Yet, they did so as citizens without calling any special attention to themselves as Jews. They were enjoying this assimilated, well-off condition when World War II burst upon them and all New Mexico. In retrospect, as memoirs and interviews indicate, the prewar era appears as a bucolic time for them.

For Jews, World War II presented a legacy of pain and raised consciousness that will remain with them throughout their history. It is difficult to imagine circumstances that can go beyond the magnitude of the horror of the concentration camps or the measure of renewed hope and fear of failure that emerged shortly after the war with the creation of the state of Israel. In the year 2000, at which time this study ends, the awareness of these events still strongly affects Jews everywhere.

Apart from these exceptional events that mark Jewish history, historians of both the United States and New Mexico regard World War II as a monumental historical marker in its own right. The role of the United States in the war, followed by its new position as a world leader, differed sharply from its earlier withdrawal from world affairs after the First World War. The immediate appearance of a new and major ideological antagonism to communism in the form of the cold war after World War II etched itself powerfully on American goals and behavior for the next half century.

These new conditions set New Mexico on a path that deflected it sharply from many of its earlier historic conditions. It became the scene for some of the most advanced scientific developments related to the war. Because of its geographic isolation, open spaces, low population density, and excellent weather, New Mexico also became a frequent site for air force training bases and arms testing.

The new economy and the population growth that accompanied it attracted a new kind of Jewish population, heavily engaged in the conditions of that new economy. These conditions mark World War II and its immediate postwar years as a new historical era for the history of New Mexico and for the Jews who selected it as their home.

CHAPTER TWO

Population Growth, 1940–2000

*O*ne factor that contributed powerfully to change in New Mexico after World War II lay in its considerable population increase. From over a half-million in 1940, the last census prior to the war, its numbers doubled by 1970, the halfway point in this study, to over a million.[1] From 1970 to the year 2000 the size of the population nearly doubled again. In the latter year New Mexico contained some 1.8 million persons.[2] For the entire period—1940–2000—the increase was somewhat over three and one-half times.

How did Jewish population figures for the state compare with its overall growth? Counting Jewish population accurately is a daunting task. One of the underlying problems of gathering such information lies in American historical reticence to inquire into the religious preferences of its citizens. The census, so valuable a source of data about American society, asks little about the faith of the country's inhabitants.

Researchers must turn to other sources to acquire knowledge of religious affiliation. The most important reliable source for identifying Jews lies in congregation membership. When dues are paid to Jewish religious institutions, for example, one feels confident in identifying the payer as Jewish. The same also applies to secular Jewish organizations. When Jewish persons choose not to join or contribute to such clearly identifiable institutions and their names do not appear on membership lists, then their discovery becomes problematic even though they may still consider themselves to be Jews. By adding institutional memberships together, as long as duplication is avoided, the researcher is left with a credible minimum figure, but one that is short of the maximum. Persons in the community with a deep interest in the size of the state's Jewish population, such as rabbis or fund-raisers, estimate that as much as 50 percent should be added to the known figures, although such guesses may leave considerable doubt.

The *American Jewish Year Book* (henceforth *AJYB*), in existence since 1899, is probably the most reliable gatherer and reporter of such data.[3] Nevertheless, its calculations depend upon information provided by local organizations—federations, religious institutions, and the like. Uncertainty remains, therefore, as to how many persons there are who do not associate with formal organizations but still consider themselves to be Jews. For gross figures of New Mexico's Jewish population we will cite the data of the *AJYB*, which at least provide a certain consistency in determining numbers.

Despite such obstacles, the Jewish population of New Mexico experienced a remarkable increase compared to the state's growth for the entire postwar period. In the years between 1940 and 2000 the percentage of the Jewish population in the state rose from 0.27 in 1940 to 0.30 in 1974, 0.40 in 1983, and 0.60 in 2000, that is, from a bit over one-quarter of 1 percent to just 0.6 of 1 percent.[4] At best, the Jewish portion still formed only a very small fraction of the state's total. Yet those increases came at a time when the population of the state was growing rapidly. One might also consider that the growth of Jewish numbers in New Mexico was occurring while the Jewish portion of the total American population was declining from 3.7 percent in 1940 to 2.2 percent in 2000.[5]

However small, and perhaps because the starting figure was so small, the increase represents a significant enlargement of the state's Jewish community. It enabled developments in organization that would have appeared unforeseeable in 1940. This development becomes evident in light of the figures of known Jews. While in 1940 the state's Jews numbered 1,179 (the same figure is used for 1937), 1960 yielded 2,700, 1981 offered 7,155, and 2000 noted 10,300.[6] One may be certain, in light of the partial data available, that the actual figures are higher. Thus, over the entire period the Jewish population grew no less than ninefold—far more impressive than the state's tripling.

A comparison of the growth of New Mexico's Jewry with that of other states from 1940 to 2000 also is impressive. In 1940, of forty-eight states, New Mexico's Jewish population ranked forty-fifth among them. By 1975 it had climbed to forty-first place out of fifty states. By 2000 it had risen to thirty-second place. Only Arizona, Florida, and Nevada had grown at a more rapid pace. Despite its still small numbers, that was no insignificant ascent in an era when the Jewish population either fell or grew modestly in many areas of the country.

Table 1 summarizes some of the above-cited data.

Table 1. Jewish Population Growth in New Mexico, 1940 to 2000

Year	Estimated No. of Jews	Total State Population	Percentage
1937	1,179	531,818	0.22
1955	1,500	781,000	0.19
1961	2,700	951,023	0.28
1970	3,645	1,006,000	0.36
1981	7,155	1,300,000	0.55
2000	10,300	1,819,000	0.60

The rate of population increase for the whole state, however noteworthy, pales when compared with its urban growth. No city matched Albuquerque's growth rate or total increase, and this was particularly so in the first decades after the war. Already the largest town in the state in 1940, long a railroad center, then a crossroad of road transportation, and finally an airport hub, its central location and physical geography allowed it to become the home of the major industries developed immediately after the war. It was also the home of the state's leading university.

From a town of 35,000 in 1940, Albuquerque grew to 200,000 by 1960—nearly a sixfold growth in twenty years.[7] By 1980 it had reached over 330,000 and in the year 2000, some 448,000.[8] For the entire period from 1940 to 2000 the city's population increased nearly thirteenfold and at the turn of the twenty-first century contained one-fourth of the state's total population.

Given the city's robust expansion and the kinds of institutions that fostered its growth, it is not surprising that the greatest increases in Jewish population also occurred in Albuquerque. In the late 1930s Albuquerque's Jews numbered about 450 and in

1970 about 2,000.[9] By the end of the century the city's estimated Jewish population stood at 7,500, having increased over sixteen-fold since 1940 and surpassing even the city's impressive rate of growth.[10] In 1940, more than 30 percent of the state's Jews lived in Albuquerque. By 1980 the urban attractions of the postwar years had raised that percentage to about 80 percent. In the last generation of the twentieth century the number of Jews in Albuquerque continued to increase but the rate of Jewish population growth of other towns may well have been greater, diminishing somewhat the city's relative portion of the state's total Jewish community. Still, in the year 2000 one could estimate that Albuquerque contained close to 70 percent of all New Mexico's Jews.

Santa Fe, the state capital, also underwent great change in the period 1940–2000. With a population of 20,000 in 1940, it had risen to over 62,000 in the year 2000—more than tripling.[11] The city's growth was rooted in reasons quite different from those driving Albuquerque's expansion. Its economic recovery after the disappearance of the Santa Fe Trail, which happened with the coming of railroads in the early 1880s, commenced solidly only in the 1920s. It was in the early twentieth century that the town began to discover and exploit the national interest in archaeology and anthropology and fascination with the nearby pueblos. That interest included the city's center, the Plaza, and the presence in it of the old Palace of the Governors. Such factors, and others as well, gave rise to a tourist industry of which Santa Fe became a major beneficiary. The fostering of Native American and Hispanic crafts and arts and a powerful campaign to restore and hold the city to a distinctive version of its regional adobe architecture rooted in the older resident cultures proved in time to be powerful national attractions. The advocates of the new trend described it as "the Santa Fe style." The Depression of the 1930s, in turn, while economically painful, nevertheless added a flood of government agencies to the state capital, giving the city its greatest growth of any decade in the twentieth century.[12]

The growing reputation of Santa Fe as a center of culture and beauty, unlike Albuquerque's military and defense industries and its educational institution, attracted its own Jewish population. In the last decades of the twentieth century its Jewish numbers grew at a pace that may have exceeded Albuquerque's. While the greatest rate of expansion in Albuquerque occurred in the first decades after the war, when the military-industrial buildup in New Mexico was at a fever pitch, Santa Fe's took place in the second half of the postwar period, when that process had already matured and begun to slow in Albuquerque.

Without a congregation as a reliable measure, one concerned old-time Santa Fe resident estimated that in 1943 there were about 30 Jewish families in the town.[13] The *AJYB* presents the figure of 75 Jews in 1940.[14] Another list, compiled by several Santa Feans in 1967, notes 207 persons, and the *AJYB* notes 260 in 1973.[15] By that time, however, a formal congregation had been established. More than half of the households in the town, by Santa Feans' recollections, were not members of the new Temple Beth Shalom.[16] In 1981 the temple's membership list alone recorded 192 households.[17] By 2001 its membership list, by household, stood at 352 and Beth Shalom was no longer the sole Jewish religious institution in the city.[18] Some estimates of total Jewish population ranged between two and three thousand, but the *AJYB* placed the number at fifteen hundred.[19] The *AJYB* figures would give Santa Fe's Jews a twentyfold increase.

Las Cruces, in south-central New Mexico, became the state's second largest city sometime after World War II. Possessing some 8,300 persons in 1940, it had expanded to over 45,000 in 1980 and reached 74,000 in 2000.[20] The reasons for its rapid early postwar growth paralleled those of Albuquerque to some extent. The development of the White Sands Proving Ground and the growth of New Mexico State University, as well as the agricultural flourishing of the Mesilla Valley, accounted heavily for its prosperity.

The presence of Jewish families in the town was not new, dating back to the mid-nineteenth century. However, like Santa Fe, Las Cruces's Jews had not created their own formal religious institutions before the war. The *AJYB* counted 34 Jews in 1940, 100 in 1973, and 600 in 2000.[21] With nearly an eighteenfold growth, the city's Jewish population lay clearly within the same range of upswing noted in Albuquerque and Santa Fe, and like those towns, surpassed sharply both the state's and the city's rate of increase.

New Mexico's postwar development expressed itself not only in the growth of older towns but also in the creation of totally new ones. The most famous, if not the largest, was Los Alamos, the center for the creation of the atomic bomb. Established by the federal government, its growth was neither the product of land development nor the function of trade routes and tourism, but the desire of the American government to achieve the results of research in relation to its perceived defense obligations in an isolated and therefore, it was hoped, secure location. While it was created as a temporary wartime facility, it became a permanent one afterward, continuing in its function as a research and development center.

The first appearance of Los Alamos in the census came in 1950. Although originally conceived as a small, elite scientific community, by 1950 it contained nearly 10,500 persons.[22] Its well-defined and regulated purpose made its growth the result of entirely different factors from those governed by the economic rules of an open society. By 1950 Los Alamos had already achieved a considerable portion of its growth for the span of years under consideration. Its greatest size thus far came in 2000 when it reached over 18,300, but that number marked little growth over its size in 1980.[23]

Jewish scientists were present at Los Alamos from its very beginning. Indeed, Jewish holiday services were practiced during the war itself. Yet, at that time of intense activity and the presence of seemingly Jewish names, as one staff member put it, "you never really knew who was Jewish."[24] Another Jewish Manhattan Project scientist, however, stated flatly that "from the beginning the percentage of Jews at Los Alamos . . . has been higher than the proportion of Jews in the general population."[25] A compilation of Jewish persons present from 1944 to 1946 included 111 names.[26] In 1991 the *AJYB* included Los Alamos as one of the state's four largest centers of Jewish population with an estimated figure of 250.[27] In the 2000 *AJYB* its ranking had fallen to fifth place (behind Taos), and its estimated numbers remained constant at 250.[28]

The last decades of the twentieth century witnessed the appearance of other new towns, such as Rio Rancho to the west and northwest of Albuquerque. It was the product of aggressive real estate development that commenced in the 1960s with a heavy early influx from the northeastern and midwestern regions of the country. As late as the mid-1980s one newspaper article commented "that Yiddish occasionally peppers supermarket conversations between shoppers."[29] In April 1981, the presentation of a Torah at the Rio Rancho Jewish Center turned out sixty families, believed to be the largest gathering to that time.[30] However, Jewish figures for the town were cloaked within the Jewish population of metropolitan Albuquerque and extremely difficult to determine. In 2002, the Jewish Community Council in Albuquerque's database listed 185 Jewish families in Rio Rancho.

In addition to new towns, the rebirth of Jewish population began in some places where their residence had long existed but had fallen off as a result of changed economic conditions. Jews in Taos, Las Vegas, and Carlsbad showed a renewed presence and energy. Toward the end of the nineteenth and in the early twentieth century Las Vegas had the largest Jewish population of any town in New Mexico. Despite having created the first congregation in the territory, however, its economic fortunes had fallen so badly by the 1930s that the congregation could no longer afford a rabbi. Indeed, the temple building itself was sold in the early 1950s to the Catholic Archdiocese of Santa Fe and served as the Newman Center for Catholic Students at New Mexico Highlands University. Jews never totally disappeared from the city, but it was only in the 1990s that organization recommenced, including town dwellers and persons from outlying communities. Residents estimated the interested at about fifty families in the late 1990s.[31]

Carlsbad, unlike Las Vegas, did not have a significant Jewish past, but Jewish families did reside there in the early twentieth century. In the postwar period they maintained a minimal presence with communal seders and celebration of the High Holy days.[32] Writing in 1988, Mark Merrian, an engineer in the nearby Waste

Isolation Pilot Plant project designed to store atomic waste, spoke of an informal congregation of twenty members that met in private homes. At that time there were no children of Hebrew school age. While a few descendants of the old families still lived there, many of the local Jewish population had come in the postwar period either for employment, to escape "big city crowding . . . in Los Angeles," or for health reasons.[33] In the mid-nineties contact with other southeastern New Mexican Jews in Roswell, Ruidoso, Alamogordo, and Hobbs led to the formation of a *chavurah* (fellowship) and the celebration of important holidays. The *Link*, the Jewish monthly journal out of Albuquerque, and the appearance of computers, no doubt, allowed an increased level of contact that would have been much more difficult to maintain a few decades earlier. The first synagogue opened in Carlsbad in 2002 with about twenty families.[34]

Taos, which had some old Jewish families such as the Gusdorfs in the territorial period, acquired a new Jewish population of artistically inclined persons, skiers, and those who sought to escape large-city life as retirees. One even finds a number of Jewish hippies, who in the late sixties dreamt of finding a utopian communal existence at what was then called New Buffalo.[35] What a change from the earliest entrepreneurial pioneers of a century earlier! In 2002 enough newcomers with sufficient interest in their common Jewishness had arrived to create a Jewish Center. Over one hundred persons attended the founding meeting. The number of Jews in the area is uncertain but local estimates presume that some five hundred live there—truly an astonishing figure, if accurate. That would place the Jewish population there among the more populous locales of Jewish settlement in the state.[36]

The *AJYB* listing of towns where Jews resided in 1940 showed no fewer than thirty-five places in New Mexico.[37] Such dispersion was indicative of the widespread merchant economy among them that existed in the prewar era. Considering that over 60 percent of the Jewish population lived outside Albuquerque in the smaller towns in 1940 and that about 10 percent resided outside of the Albuquerque–Santa Fe area in 2000, the path of Jewish urbanization is quite clear. Nevertheless, the creation of new or regenerated centers in the last generation of the twentieth century seems to soften to some extent the major industrial and cultural urbanization of the Jewish population in New Mexico. The rapid Jewish population growth accommodated both urban growth and small-town residence.

CHAPTER THREE

Social and Economic Change

$\mathcal{F}$or New Mexico, the war produced changes that dramatically altered its economic and social complexion. One early and strong component of those changes lay in the new purposes that the federal government introduced during the war and the continued and strengthened support of those purposes after the war. The new research and development facilities that it created or supported required a type of educated work force that could not be recruited within the state. Engineers, scientists, and professionally trained technicians were the keys to fulfilling the needs of the new establishments.

The clearest and most extreme example of this change, although not the largest, was in the creation of Los Alamos. While one may speak of it as a wartime project, after the war's end it turned into a "company" town that only partially opened its gates to the public in 1957. By 1960 the town's population exceeded 12,500. The National Laboratory itself employed some 7,700 persons, more than 1,500 of them PhDs.[1]

From its very beginning, this extraordinary community contained a considerable Jewish population. Some of the most important early figures in the Manhattan Project to build the atomic bomb who moved to the state, at least temporarily, were Jews, including its scientific director J. Robert Oppenheimer. It was he who had recommended the site to General Leslie Groves, the head of the project. The site was known to him through early childhood visits to the area. Other leading figures among the scientists, such as Leo Szilard and Edward Teller, were also Jews. There is evidence that the Jewish personnel had a common interest in maintaining their identity. Despite a rigorous work schedule, they seemed to find each other. Some took part in holiday services during the war itself. Here was a new population of Jewish engineers and physicists unknown by education within the New Mexican Jewish population before World War II.

Albuquerque also heavily reflected the effects of this new sort of growth. Institutions with close ties to Los Alamos, such as the Sandia Corporation, became major employers in the town. In 1949 over 1,700 Albuquerqueans were employed there and in 1955 some 5,700.[2] One-fourth of its employees held college degrees. Jewish scientists and engineers joined their number, contributing to the change in the economic and social makeup of the local Jewish population. Albuquerque in 1960 claimed the highest number of PhDs per capita in the United States.[3]

In a broader perspective, the federal government created other policies in the immediate postwar period that impacted older institutions in favor of persons having or seeking higher education. The GI Bill, for example, granted financial aid to countless numbers of veterans to enable them to gain a higher education. Its effects quickly altered the University of New Mexico. In 1945 its student population had reached a low of 600, largely due to the effects of the military draft. By the fall of 1949, however, the university's enrollment had leaped to 5,700. After some years of stabilization its numbers climbed again to 13,000 in the late 1960s and to 26,000 in the early 1990s. By that time, with 12,000 employees, the university had become the largest employer in the state. Moreover, degree programs expanded with numbers. Before the 1970s new graduate schools in law and medicine had been added.[4]

With the growth of new programs came Jewish students and faculty members. An attempted compilation of the latter in 1977 listed 98 Jewish faculty—41 in the medical school alone![5] In the arts and sciences Jewish faculty participated across a broad spectrum of disciplines. In the early 1970s estimates of Jewish students ran to 400.[6] By that time the Jewish population of the university, faculty, and students, neared what had been the total Jewish numbers of the entire city in 1940.

After 1981, Rio Rancho, across the river from Albuquerque, gained the presence of Intel, one of the largest semiconductor manufacturing plants in the world. By 1990 it had more than 1,300 employees, and in the later nineties, more than 3,000. One group of temporary newcomers to the plant in the nineties rates special, if passing, mention—the Israelis in training for two-year terms. In 1998 they, with their relatives, comprised some 100 families. The trainees were brought to the Albuquerque area to acquire the technical knowledge needed for a new Intel plant scheduled to open in Israel in 1999. Cultural differences, as well as their intent to return to their homeland, tended to keep them apart from the permanent residents.[7]

The new Jewish population of professionals formed a significant segment of this new sort of immigrant to New Mexico. They were often the second- and third-generation descendants of the flood of immigrants from Eastern Europe who had come to the United States from the late nineteenth century to the early 1920s. Despite some obstacles that had inhibited their free entry to technical education before the war, Jewish students flocked to universities with a persistence and dedication and in numbers that were remarkable. By 1947, 62 percent of college-age Jews in the United States were enrolled in institutions of higher education.[8]

The educational level of Albuquerque's Jews reflected what was taking place nationally. The younger the person, the more certain it was that he had achieved a higher level of education than persons of earlier generations. By 1980, 93 percent of those in their thirties had acquired some level of higher education. Only half that percentage could have made that claim in the 1950s.[9] How much higher could the figure go in the last generation of the century?

The type of employment required in the above-mentioned new institutions sharply altered how a considerable portion of the Jewish community in New Mexico earned its livelihood. An early example of such change appears through an examination of the records of Albuquerque's Congregation B'nai Israel. A listing of its membership in 1941, a few months prior to the American entry into World War II, reveals that of fifty-four clearly identified persons (out of sixty), forty-two were proprietors—80 percent. The remainder worked as salesmen or clerks, a teacher, a doctor, and a manager.[10] B'nai Israel's Jews at that time formed about as solid and classic a traditional middle-class community as one could conceive. By way of comparison, early Los Alamos displayed an absence of entrepreneurs.

Roughly a quarter-century later, in 1965, B'nai Israel's membership had risen to 242, a fourfold increase. About half of the sixty persons listed in 1941 still appeared in the 1965 roll. To measure the changes in terms of new arrivals, these "old-timers" were separated from the list of newcomers, the vast majority of whom joined after 1945.[11] The clearest changes in how they made their livelihood are reflected in the fact that only 27 percent of the newcomers were entrepreneurs. In their stead, a second category, almost as large as the share held by entrepreneurs, had joined the congregation, composed of medical doctors, dentists, engineers, faculty members, attorneys, and professionally degreed persons ranging from architects to pharmacists. Salespersons, teachers, government employees (including military personnel), managers, and retirees made up the bulk of the rest. The range of employment had broadened greatly and many of the newcomers were no longer of the entrepreneurial definition of middle class even though one could scarcely categorize them as either very rich or working-class poor in terms of income.

Another body of evidence that allows an early and late postwar comparison of economic life in Albuquerque lies in the membership of Albuquerque's Congregation Albert. It was also the only other functioning congregation in New Mexico before World War II, as well as the largest and the oldest. Extant documentation, however, allows for only an early postwar listing of membership to be compared with the lists of later decades. The membership list of 1950–51 showed 44 percent as proprietors and 21 percent as professionally degreed. Nearly 10 percent of the employed membership were medical doctors.[12] Despite the inability to make comparisons with earlier lists, it is clear that the highly degreed professionals already had made a significant appearance.

The middle years of the postwar era—from 1955 to 1984—demonstrate the continuation of the already visible trend in occupational change among Albuquerque's Jews. Table 2 below includes data derived from both congregations and a Jewish Welfare Fund survey conducted in 1966.[13] The increase of Jewish professionals in Albuquerque displayed particular strength in the fields of medicine and law. In Congregation Albert alone, in 1965 doctors formed over 10 percent of the working membership and attorneys close to 6 percent. By 1984 these shares had risen only slightly in a rapidly growing congregation membership. Yet, in the year 2000, out of 606 working members more than 14 percent were doctors and close to 9 percent attorneys—just under one-fourth of the working population.[14] Truly an impressive figure!

Table 2 summarizes the changes in occupation. The numbers of persons included form a considerable percentage of the total working Jewish population in Albuquerque. The data comprise

Table 2. Occupational Distribution in Percentages of the Jewish Population in Albuquerque, 1955–2000

Occupation	1955	1965	1984	2000
Professionals	16.1	21.4	38.4	45.0
Technicians	9.1	6.4	4.6	3.5
Subtotal	25.2	27.8	43.0	48.5
Managers	15.8	12.8	10.5	7.0
Sales	12.3	9.3	8.9	4.2
Proprietors	40.1	29.5	20.8	9.2
Subtotal	68.2	51.6	40.2	20.4
Total	93.4	79.4	83.2	68.9

more than a sample even though they lack the certainty that would accompany a census-derived compilation. The latter, however, is not available.

By the early eighties, those employed in professional and technical fields had outdistanced those engaged in any kind of commercial trade—either in sales or direct ownership. Indeed, the percentage of professionals nearly doubled that of proprietors. Many of the trends witnessed since World War II continued to the year 2000 although some changes of definition of proprietorship are in order. Self-employed persons were included under proprietorships. A major category of persons not considered in the table was retirees.

The rapid changes in the composition of the Jewish population and the new conditions created by the war offer grounds for a comparison between the prewar Jewish community and the one that emerged in the postwar years. Jews born and raised in New Mexico in the prewar era usually portray the environment in favorable terms for Jews. The settled character of the older New Mexico families, abetted by slow population growth, allowed for a homogeneity among the local Jews and a successful accommodation with the surrounding culture. Only in the late 1930s did a few newcomers escaping from unsettled European conditions begin to flavor the New Mexico scene.

New Mexico's Jewish environment differed considerably from that of Jews in northeastern cities. New York, for instance, for all its purported "melting pot" character, could be better described as a "stewpot" that contained cultural differences of every imaginable kind within itself. There, a population fed by a heavy and continuous stream of immigrants from Europe existed until the mid-1920s, when national legislation sharply reduced the flow. The kind of cultural accommodation that was already well along in New Mexico was still one or two generations away.

Jews in New Mexico were accustomed to the presence of a large Hispanic population in which Spanish language usage and the dominating presence of the Catholic Church were major factors of identification. From their earliest appearance in New Mexico, Jews learned Spanish as a second-language business necessity and as a social inevitability. However, even the religious distinctions between Catholic and Jew in New Mexico were often gentle as a result of long contact between populations accustomed to each other's presence. The small Jewish population offered no threat to the Catholic Church. Indeed, the potential and actuality of religious difference in New Mexico expressed itself in more antagonistic terms between Protestant groups and the Catholic Church than between Jews and Christians.

In New York, by comparison, the recent European backgrounds and cultural baggage each group carried to America permitted the animosities of the Old World to migrate with them even though the new environment reduced their potency. Cultural differences between Italians, Irish, Polish, and Yiddish-speaking Jews allowed the gaps between those populations to be more acerbic than cultural distinctions in New Mexico.

The postwar Jewish immigration to New Mexico required less need to adapt to the heavily Hispanic population than the prewar New Mexican Jewish population. Filling positions in medicine, higher education, and new technological institutions, they were not tied to the business expectations of the older Jewish merchants who relied on Hispanics as customers. The newcomers could just as easily expect the Hispanics to adjust to the new modern American culture they brought with them.

Among Jews themselves conditions in the East differed from those in New Mexico. Much of the variety of ideological positions—secular and religious—that existed in New York was simply absent in New Mexico before the war. Jewish labor and socialist organizations, for instance, found no equivalent in New Mexico. In New York, before World War II, Jewish tailor unionists battled Jewish entrepreneurs in that city's clothing industry. Orthodox Jews and secular and even atheist Jews had to deal with each other as well. Such distinctions scarcely existed in New Mexico. Assimilation, economic homogeneity, and family ties had already done their work on the older, more settled New Mexican Jewish population.

There were also factors that made continuing Jewish unity in New Mexico easier to attain than in New York. The postwar newcomers to New Mexico were not a foreign immigrant population. They may have differed somewhat from the old local population in the level of their formal education and occupations, but they displayed the results of their American education. In that sense, they could blend readily with the already assimilated older New Mexican Jewish population. Moreover, in the early decades after the war the paucity of Jewish organization in New Mexico brought old and new populations into the same few institutions, a phenomenon that did not occur in northeastern cities where the variety of organizations was legion. The new issues affecting all Jews that arose out of the war produced strong common purpose and sharpness of focus nationally despite any local social differences.

Changes in the economy of New Mexico marked the last twenty years of the century. By far the greatest single increase came in the service sector. Although manufacturing increased with the creation of such industries as Intel, the service sector, with health services leading the way, jumped, as witnessed by increased employment.[15] Jewish institutions catering to the service needs of the population grew. The creation of the Jewish Family Service and the home for the well elderly are prime examples. Yet the inclusion of government funds to such institutions required that they provide their expertise and resources to the entire population, not only to Jews. In a sense, the social expansion of the Jewish community forced it to lose some of the separateness that was an integral part of purely religious institutions.

The last generation of the twentieth century, 1980 to 2000, also witnessed significant changes of a different sort. In the earlier decades, many of the newcomers raised and educated elsewhere in the United States were relatively young and had come to practice their skills in New Mexico. However, by 1980 the rapid economic expansion of the earlier postwar decades had passed its time of greatest growth. With the passage of decades, the defense industries had matured and the population had aged, with retirement becoming an increasingly evident fact of life. The number of single-person households grew as death claimed one adult member of an original family where there had been two. New Mexico also became an increasingly favorable location for newcomers who had already retired.

The aging process, as illustrated in the membership of Albuquerque's B'nai Israel, demonstrates the trend. In 1980 about

20 percent of the family memberships appeared as retired. In the year 2000 the retirees' share had risen to about 33 percent of the total membership. The newcomers to the congregation, that is, those who joined between 1980 and 2000 alone, showed about 25 percent as retirees.[16] The count seems to confirm that not only was the existing 1980 membership growing older, but that an older Jewish population was making its way to New Mexico.

Santa Fe, with its own unique reasons for growth, also experienced its own unique social changes within its Jewish population. In 1968, not unlike Albuquerque a generation earlier, old storefront proprietors still comprised 40 percent of its working force, judging by Temple Beth Shalom's membership.[17] But professionalization had also affected the town, Jewish doctors alone comprising 19 percent of the Jewish working population, approximating the percentage of Albuquerque's Jewish professional population. Beyond that, 60 percent of Santa Fe's professional Jewish population included a scattering of attorneys, engineers, physicists (often commuters to Los Alamos), teachers, and government employees.

With its greater growth coming in later decades after the war as compared with Albuquerque, the social changes in Santa Fe also reflected themselves later. By 1981 Congregation Beth Shalom's membership had more than quadrupled over 1968. Clearly, much of this population was new to Santa Fe and the newcomers reflected the changing economic environment of the city. Only a handful of the old stores present in 1968 still existed in 1981. Retirement accounted for much of their disappearance. There were also entrepreneurs among the new members, that is, those who joined between 1968 and 1981, but the rapid growth of the congregation reduced the percentage of entrepreneurs from its previous 40 percent to about 18 percent.[18] Many of the newcomer-entrepreneurs presented different areas of livelihood from the storekeepers. There were restaurateurs, investment counselors, art gallery owners, and nursing home owners. The spread reflected the changing economy of the city with its growing arts population, its retirees, and the rising importance of tourism.

While those described as proprietors or high-ranking executives still formed the largest single contingent in 1981, the second highest grouping became retirees. By the early eighties, despite its rising cost of living, Santa Fe's cultural charms were attracting them in considerable numbers. Medical doctors fell as a percentage, but if one added attorneys, then professionals comprised an even larger share than proprietors. The prewar presence of Jews as store proprietors in Santa Fe had diminished in favor of the new direction that the economy was moving.

Other social changes that loomed large on the American social canvas also displayed themselves in the Jewish population. The rise of the women's movement in the 1960s and the accompanying increase in women's expectations were notable within the Jewish community. Perhaps the sharpest change appeared in their level of education. While by 1981 somewhat over one-third of Jewish females in Albuquerque over the age of thirty had acquired undergraduate degrees, roughly the same proportion as those over age sixty, those attaining graduate or professional degrees showed a sharp increase. Only 11 percent of Jewish women over sixty had achieved that goal in 1981. Of those between the ages of thirty-one and forty, however, some 47 percent had completed advanced degrees, a dramatic change reflecting new attitudes toward careers.[19] The assumed place of males as the sole breadwinners gradually gave way to the two-person working family. Divorce, too, became an unavoidable consideration shaping Jewish social composition just as its presence increased in the general population.

Changing attitudes found their way into the major congregations. Feminism showed great strength in the Jewish population. In the late 1970s B'nai Israel elected a woman president, Marilyn Reinman. Congregation Albert had chosen that path slightly earlier, electing Mrs. Stuart Cahn in 1975. The practice became quite common in the 1990s in both congregations.

The power of feminism also showed itself through changes of style in name usage in the period 1980–2000. Congregation Albert's membership in 1980 showed only two households with different or hyphenated last names. In 2000, however, over 10 percent of the total membership of the congregation used different or hyphenated names.[20] Congregation B'nai Israel's members showed a similar but not as strong a trend in those years. Perhaps the more traditional nature of its membership accounts for the lesser usage of the new name style. Yet the change is significant since the two congregations together may have included as much as one-third of the total Jewish population of Albuquerque.

Santa Fe's differing social characteristics, as displayed in the membership of Temple Beth Shalom, further emphasizes the power of the feminist trend. While the name style changes had barely appeared in 1980, in 2001 close to 25 percent of the congregation were employing this sign of changing self-identification.[21] The usage of the style seems to affirm the attraction of feminism in the largest and most liberal Jewish congregations.

Single-person household memberships at Santa Fe's Beth Shalom remained fairly stable between 1980 and 2000, declining slightly from 40 to 36 percent. However, the single-female household membership expanded greatly. In 1981 single-female households exceeded their single-male equivalents by fewer than two to one. By 2001, however, there were over three times as many single-female households compared to those of males in the congregation. Of the new single-member households who joined between 1980 and 2000, the ratio of female households to male was approaching four to one—an astonishing change it would appear.[22] Santa Fe's cultural attractions probably contributed heavily to the change.

Congregation Albert in Albuquerque displayed a similar trend although not quite as pronounced. In 1971 there were as many single-household males as females. In 1980, single-female household memberships favored women nearly three to one. In 2000, however, that ratio declined slightly to about two and a half times to one in favor of single-named female memberships. Of new single-household names that appeared in 2000, the female-to-male ratio was about the same.[23]

The last generation of the century also witnessed the results of the powerful changes of attitude among women toward work. With higher education open to them as never before, Jewish women sought and completed professional education in far greater numbers than could have been conceivable in the early decades after the war. For example, there were virtually no female attorneys in the mid-1960s in Albuquerque's two largest congregations. Even in 1980 there were only a handful, possibly a little over 10 percent of the total number of Jewish lawyers. By the year 2000, however, about one-third of the profession was female in the aggregate figure for both congregations.[24]

A comparison of the prewar history of the Jewish social scene in New Mexico with the post–World War II era shows clearly the sharp difference between the two. From a population in the nineteenth century where Jewish women were scarce and Jewish men of means went back to the Old Country or to the eastern United States to find Jewish wives, the women had moved into an occupational visibility and independence that began to match male activity in every respect. One may suggest that the occupational status of Jewish women was nearly the opposite by 2000 of what it had been in 1900. This social change was one of the greatest that occurred within Jewish society in New Mexico, and the changes were strongest in the last generation of the century.

New factors also produced changes in the sociocultural nature of Jewish life—sometimes with special force in the still sparse Jewish population of New Mexico. A study of intermarriage among Jews in the United States reported in the early 1970s that before the 1960s there was a prevailing rate of 12 percent. In that decade, however, the rate began to climb rapidly, reaching 30 percent in the first half of the sixties and an astonishing 48 percent by the seventies. In 75 percent of these cases it was the Jewish male who married a non-Jewish female. Over one-fourth of these non-Jewish wives converted to Judaism.[25] Scholarly studies confirm the rising trend of intermarriage in those decades.[26] Such a new direction produced a powerful and broad impact on the nature of the Jewish population.

In general, the religious leaders of Judaism, as of other faiths, have usually discouraged intermarriage. They saw in it a dilution of Judaism that could easily weaken the already small numbers of Jews in the population at large. The rate of intermarriage in the middle decades of nineteenth-century New Mexico appeared to be the result of the small numbers of single Jewish women available. Yet despite the sharp increase of Jewish population in the postwar era there was a similarly large increase in mixed marriages.

The cause of this new increase appeared to be the result of the marked social changes that brought a new openness to American society in general. One could argue that the Jews gained fuller entry into American society through assimilation and education and that increased intermarriage resulted from that desirable condition of greater acceptance.[27] The increase must also be measured against the impressive growth of Jewish religious and secular organizations.

In the first decades after World War II, intermarriage performed by a Jewish clergyman was still not easy to achieve in New Mexico. Rabbi Abraham Shinedling, a Reform rabbi who lived in Albuquerque and was virtually retired in the 1960s but nevertheless still performed a variety of rabbinical services, wrote an unpublished paper on the subject in 1967. His love of baseball earned him the sobriquet "rabbinical pinch hitter." He described himself as "the only rabbi . . . in this entire southwestern territory of some several hundred thousand square miles . . . who is willing to officiate at marriages of Jewish partners to non-Jewish partners."[28] His nearly half century experience as a rabbi led him to a conclusion that matched scholarly studies, which gave a national picture of predominantly Jewish males marrying non-Jewish women. His Albuquerque contemporaries at Congregation Albert (Rabbi David Shor) and B'nai

Israel (Rabbi Yisroel Klein), he noted, did not perform such marriage ceremonies.[29] Clearly, intermarriage via Jewish clergy was not the only way such unions could occur.

There is no great abundance of studies on intermarriage in the United States. A report on the western region sponsored by the Council of Jewish Federations in 1994 described a higher rate of mixed marriages there than in any other region of the country. The lowest rate lay in the Northeast (28 percent), and the highest in the West (38 percent).[30]

Some fragmentary evidence does exist, however, for New Mexico itself. One doctoral dissertation, concentrating on facets of Albuquerque Jewry in the early eighties, compared intermarriage in that city (and Denver) with intermarriage in large eastern centers. The western cities, the author believed, showed much higher rates of intermarriage. The relatively small numbers who came and the resulting dilution of population as well as the possibility that persons less than totally committed to Judaism moved here in the first place, the author speculated, might well account for the high intermarriage rate.[31] In 1984 the author placed the rate of intermarriage in her sample at 31 percent. However, over 30 percent of the non-Jewish spouses converted to Judaism.[32]

A count made at Santa Fe's Temple Beth Shalom of mixed marriages in 1988 provides a glimpse into that community's state of intermarriage. About fifty such marriages and relationships out of a membership of nearly three hundred would indicate that approximately 17 percent of the congregation were intermarried.[33] It may well be that the large numbers of Jews not belonging to any formal religious institution in the last two decades of the twentieth century might provide a much higher figure.

The changes in New Mexican Jewish society brought its social and economic composition much closer to the general appearance of American Jewish society. It expanded from a narrow range of entrepreneurship into a broader range that included a strong professional presence. As American society moved from a dominant male presence into one that included women, Jewish society moved alongside it. Although always urban in residence, they moved more heavily toward that posture, as did American society in general. If Jews did not become more agricultural in their activity, neither did America. Yet both in America and in New Mexico, the Jews had not become a statistical mirror image of the larger society even if they moved closer to it.

The largest of the Jewish communities in the state—Albuquerque and Santa Fe—no longer resembled the frontier and small-town character that had persisted until World War II. Perhaps the greatest change was the one summarized by American-Jewish historian Howard M. Sachar, who wrote in 2005 that "the third and fourth generations of American Jews craved a soul-satisfying blend of economic security and intellectual activity."[34] In New Mexico, one might add, with its high degree of religious openness and expanding opportunities for economic participation, Jews became participating citizens in a broader spectrum of society as never before.

CHAPTER FOUR

The Growth of Secular Organizations

$\mathcal{T}$he earliest Jewish religious and social organizations came into existence in New Mexico in the 1880s—about forty years after the first Ashkenazic Jews settled in the new American territory. However, it was nearly a century after their original arrival before national secular organizations began to make a serious mark on the New Mexico Jewish population. The events of World War II and the immediate postwar years drew these Jews out of the isolation that so long surrounded them by virtue of New Mexico's geographic location. Their strong assimilation and small numbers offered grounds for the relative absence of concern with the larger American Jewish world, although individuals did contribute to broader causes. Attachment to extended family and business concerns, as well as local issues, for the most part seemed to satisfy their social needs as Jews and citizens. However, it should be noted that students of Jewish organization in the United States have found that, in general, a significant minority of American Jews long remained apart from larger group endeavors.[1] This separation may have been particularly true in areas where Jewish numbers were small. With new post–World War II issues and perspectives and a rapidly growing and changing population, New Mexico's Jews began to move beyond their prewar condition into closer contact with other Jews both locally and nationally.

Before the United States entered the war, an *American Jewish Year Book* list of Jewish national organizations occupied sixty-eight pages of text. They ranged from educational and youth organizations (e.g., Hillel at universities) to ethnic groups (e.g., Council of Roumanian Jews), to labor-oriented organizations (e.g., Jewish Labor Committee), to professional organizations (e.g., Jewish Physicians Committee), Zionist organizations, and to the organizations of the religious branches of Judaism.[2] Given prewar New Mexican Jewry's narrow cultural, social, and economic base and its relative uniformity, as well as the state's geographic isolation, the absence of a broad spectrum of Jewish organizations such as existed in large centers where recent European immigration had been the rule for nearly a half century was understandable.

In prewar New Mexico, religious congregations and their internal offshoots, such as sisterhoods, comprised virtually the only dimensions of organization. B'nai B'rith was the sole notable noncongregational exception. After the war a new array of secular demands that affected all Jews arose alongside the traditional religious ones. The change reflected the powerful awareness of the painful condition of Jews elsewhere and the felt obligation to organize locally to aid their brethren. American Jews in general also had to consider their own condition within the context of change. By the year 2000 the range of activities had expanded sharply in New Mexico, reflecting the growth of the population and their interests and needs. Whereas before World War II New Mexican Jews had sought to fit into the local culture in which they lived, the new set of conditions added a strong dimension of concern with the fate of the outside Jewish world as well as with the continuing issue of adapting themselves to New Mexico.

The same *American Jewish Year Book* that listed the plethora of Jewish national organizations prior to World War II noted only one for New Mexico in 1938—the Federation of Jewish Charities (Albuquerque and vicinity)—with Leopold Meyer as its chairman.[3] The *AJYB* might have added others, such as the Zionist Organization of America, which had old roots among members of Congregation B'nai Israel.[4] The year 1948 saw the formal establishment of a new secular organization when the Albuquerque Jewish Welfare Fund (AJWF) incorporated itself, although it had organized informally several years earlier.[5] The efforts of its fund-raising went primarily to the United Jewish Appeal (UJA), a national organization that had been created in 1939 out of several Jewish organizations to deal solely with the collection and distribution of funds for local, national, and international purposes. By that action the AJWF linked itself with the single American Jewish fund-raising organization for relief work in Europe, for immigration to and settlement in Palestine, and for refugee aid in the United States.[6]

Over the half century since World War II the response of New Mexico's Jews to the requests for funds grew considerably. During the first five years of the postwar period (1946–50) the AJWF collected a total of $150,000. A decade later, in 1960 alone, the campaign for funds brought in $73,000. For 1970 the fund-raising effort more than doubled to $158,000. For 1980 the approved budget reached more than $301,000, that of 1990 some $454,000, and for the year 2000, $768,000.[7] The pace of fund-raising for the post-war half century was clearly one of rapid and strong increase but somewhat short of keeping up with the growth rate of the state's Jewish population.

The UJA, from the beginning, became the largest single benefi-ciary of fund-raising in Albuquerque. Even before the official cre-ation of the AJWF in 1948, it had given $1,000 to the UJA. By 1950, out of a total of the nearly $150,000 collected for the years 1946 to 1950, $113,000—three-fourths of the total—had reached the UJA.[8] The early presidents recall that the monies collected went largely to aid Israel.[9]

A new culture of involvement in secular issues of importance to Jews grew up, augmenting the activities that had been virtually the sole province of the religious congregations. Even in the late 1940s, when so much of the funds collected went to the UJA, the AJWF contributed minor sums to educational institutions such as the Weizman Institute of Science, the Jewish Braille Institute, the Jewish Theological Seminary, Yeshiva University; to Jewish hos-pitals looking after Jewish orphans; and to Jewish defense orga-nizations, some forty-seven in all. However, small as some of the allocations were, they indicated a growing spectrum of local inter-est in national American Jewish life. Even the Hillel Foundation, the student organization at the University of New Mexico, where the number of Jewish students was growing, began receiving funds in 1949.[10]

The new interest in secular organizations necessitated the cre-ation of a new cadre of persons separate from the religious con-gregations, although many of these activists participated in both sectors of activity. The campaigns for funds gradually became an organizational focal point of community life. Over the decades the activists produced a list of names that recurred again and again as presidents and general campaign and women's campaign leaders. In the early decades after the war, through the seventies, Yale Weinstein, Kurt Kubie, Milton Seligman, several generations of the Sutin family (Lewis and then Michael and Jonathan Sutin), and

FIGURE 1. Lewis Sutin. Courtesy of Michael Sutin.

Harold and next-generation Judy and Arthur Gardenswartz performed exceptional service. In the eighties and nineties Miriam Efroymson, Shirlee Londer, Harold Albert, and Keith Harvie joined a list far too lengthy to produce to do justice to all.

One notable person among the many admirable activists of the early postwar decades was Rana Adler, the executive secretary of

FIGURE 2. Michael Sutin. Courtesy of Michael Sutin.

the AJWF, who served from 1951 to 1970. She might be considered the first secular community professional—at least on a part-time basis. Her concern for the early refugee families who arrived in New Mexico after the war under JWF sponsorship was exceptional.[11]

How well Albuquerque's efforts compared with those of other American communities in its funding and participation in secular Jewish activity is difficult to calculate. It may be that the unusually large influx of new population during the first postwar decades

FIGURE 3. Rana Adler. Courtesy of Judy Felsen.

exceeded the capabilities of the developing organizations to include them efficiently or for the newcomers to adapt readily to the circumstances of New Mexico. A report by the executive directors of Albuquerque's Welfare Fund, who attended a conference of directors in Los Angeles in 1967, lamented that the size of income produced by campaigns and the absence of institutions for the ill or elderly and a community center left Albuquerque's delegates with little room to participate in discussions.[12]

Later that year, Michael Sutin, in his presidential remarks at the AJWF annual meeting, pointedly indicated that Albuquerque's Jews still did not act as a community except for their response to Israeli emergencies. The AJWF, he contended, merely raised and disbursed monies while the Jewish population did not urge its leaders toward national programming.[13]

Even in 1981 an evaluation of the Jewish Community Council of Albuquerque (JCCA) drew criticism when an outside evaluator, M. C. Gettinger, compared the size of the city's Jewish population and the variety of services offered to that of other towns. Among the eleven towns he offered for comparison (among which Albuquerque's 6,500 Jews had the largest population), its campaigns netted far less, its per capita donations amounted to considerably less, and even its largest gift donors ranked far below those of other towns. He estimated that one of three households had made pledges in 1980 whereas half or more had done so in the comparable towns. Perhaps most telling with respect to the level of the Albuquerqueans' performance was his demonstration that they gave $46 per capita while the next lowest town, El Paso, gave $131 per person—about three times as much.[14] And this was in a town whose Jewish population, if not wealthy, was far from poverty-stricken!

However, some matters were already changing by 1981. In 1972 AJWF changed its name to the Jewish Community Council of Albuquerque (JCCA). Then-president Yale Weinstein disliked the connotation of the term "welfare" and the fact that so much of the funding still went to Israel.[15] A number of Jewish organizations and programs had emerged since 1948, among them a day camp (later Gan), the Israel Day celebration, the Experiment in Jewish Learning, and the goal of creating an Albuquerque Home for the Aged. Yet it appeared at times that the support each program received from the Welfare Fund depended on pressure exerted by contributors to the fund. Individual organizations, one member noted, showed interest only in their own activities; they were not inclusive.[16] Michael G. Sutin, by then a past president of the fund, felt that its approach tended to fragment the community.[17] The road to a better Jewish community, he argued, lay in a more open and inclusive organizational form and one that took responsibility for programs that it funded.[18] The growing complexity of the fund's affairs had even led to the hiring of a professional executive director in 1971 after the retirement of long-term part-time director Rana Adler. The name change expressed the need for greater coordination and unity than had been achieved up to that time. By the turn of the new century, however, the scope of services available to the Jewish population, according to the then administrative leader of the federation, Andrew Lipman, had reached a level of organizational growth in line with other cities of Albuquerque's size.[19]

Perhaps the surest sign of organizational consolidation came in the joining of the Home for the Jewish Aged project and the JCCA. The effort to create the institution had begun in the early

1960s, when, under the passionate driving force of David Specter, a ten-acre plot of land was purchased for the purpose of locating the institution. The AJWF contributed funds regularly for the purchase of the land.[20] The actual merger of the two came about in 1973.[21] The realization of a brick-and-mortar facility, however, still lay a number of years in the future.

The early seventies also witnessed the growth of outreach between the organization and the general Jewish population. In 1971 the mailing list of the JCCA included some 700 families. Three years later, in 1974, it counted some 1,500 families.[22] That increase represented a growing interest of Albuquerque's Jews to be part of a community, and the existence of an agency to bind them together— a condition that had been lacking in earlier decades.

In June 1984, organization of the Jewish community underwent another name change. The JCCA became the Jewish Federation of Greater Albuquerque (JFGA). The change reflected the great organizational expansion that was taking place. It placed New Mexico, and the Albuquerque area in particular, on a level with other federations across the country in its form and functions.[23]

The variety of issues that concerned the community led at times to friction with respect to priorities. For example, the need to support Israel competed with the growth of local community needs, such as proper planning for senior citizens—a growing concern— and the perceived desire to create a community center.[24] Education for Jewish children also involved differences between the role of religious congregations and of a secular community institution.[25] In 1960 the range of allocations extended from over half of the funds (over $49,000) going to the UJA, to the next largest sums, $2,000 each, for the Joint Defense Appeal and local and transient aid, to as low as $25 for YIVO (Yiddish Scientific Institute) and the Synagogue Council of America. Some thirty-nine agencies and institutions were listed as beneficiaries independent of administrative expenses (which consumed nearly 10 percent of the total allocations of $73,000 and of reserve funds).[26]

FIGURE 4. Elisa Simon, prominent social work activist.
Courtesy of the *Link*.

The increasing complexity of local affairs received an added presence in 1985 when the Jewish Family Service was established—a sign of recognition that problems of family, aging, and even financial security less known in earlier times needed professional attention. The new agency concentrated on aiding the elderly, single parents, children (out of which adolescent children formed a considerable segment), and immigrants. It even sought to provide short-term financial help when necessary.[27] The agency also sponsored Russian immigrant families who moved into the area.[28] Not that these services were ignored earlier. Elisa Simon, who became a major figure throughout the eighties in dealing with social welfare problems, noted that she was hired in 1978 on a one-day-a-week basis to deal with them. Prior to that, she observed, the belief existed "that there were no people (Jews) in need here."[29] After 1985, however, the weight of these problems demanded and received a visible agency of its own. Under the early leadership of Beatrice Bittner, followed by Art Fine (who at this time of writing still leads the organization), the Jewish Family Service continued to broaden its area of concern.

Concern over the fate of Israel proved especially powerful in times of crisis. The year 1967 witnessed Israel at war against its Arab neighbors and allocations responded to the circumstances. While the regular fund-raising campaign produced over $75,000, the vision of an endangered Israel led to the creation of an emergency fund that more then doubled the entire allocation ($157,000) for the year.[30] It should be noted that approximately one-fourth of the contributors to the 1967 emergency fund were not Jews.[31] A similar pattern followed the Yom Kippur War in 1973.

Even without wartime crises in Israel, the commitment of funds to its needs usually remained the largest item of allocation. For the entire postwar period, however, there was a gradual, but uneven, reduction in how much of the budget the new Jewish state and overseas problems consumed. Starting with 75 percent for the 1947–50 years, the allocation declined to 68 percent in 1957–58, 28 percent in 1970–71, 44 percent in 1980, 33 percent in 1990, and 19 percent in 2000.[32]

By contrast, concern with local issues increasingly showed their presence in the budgets of the federation. As noted, such concerns as the work of Jewish Family Service, created in 1985, were virtually absent in 1970 but consumed over 16 percent in 1990. The increasing complexity of the Community Council also made itself felt. In 1957–58 some 13 percent of the budget went to its purposes. A considerable jump occurred in the early seventies when professionalization of administration took place. In 1971–72 administrative needs had risen to 20 percent.

Over the years, the desire for a campus to attend to the needs of the whole community took on added importance. It already had been a subject of discussion in 1959.[33] Decades passed, however, before a facility to accommodate local needs became a concrete possibility. In the early nineties a community survey revealed a positive attitude toward the creation of a community center.[34] In the evaluation of its assessor at that time, the highest priority revolved around the need to reach out to teenagers—to increase the options open to them where small numbers "and ease of freedom to use the general community" lowered the place of Jewishness in their perspective.[35] The survey saw a major avenue for improvement in the sense of community for both youth and adults in the creation of sports and fitness facilities. Indeed, to succeed, the report concluded, "we will have to build a *first class fitness facility.*"[36]

Beyond that, the need for adult meeting space and quality programs to attract young professionals—potential leaders—and, hopefully, financial contributors, ranked high in the assessment. The programs suggested through the survey ranged from topics such as divorce, single parenthood, and connecting with teens to forums dealing with social issues of importance to Jews. The spectrum of concerns was as broad as life itself.

On a practical level, by the late eighties a number of large donations became available, which made the creation of a community facility a practical reality. The Gardenswartz family donated $375,000 in 1987, Abe and Sophia Cohen contributed a half-million in the mid-nineties, and the major contributions of Florence Gusowsky and the Harry and Jeanette Weinberg Foundation finally provided the boost that enabled the formulation and completion of the Jewish Community Center in the year 2000.[37]

In November of that year, the Jewish community organization attained its long-held dream. It opened a campus that housed not only the administrative offices of the center but included a gymnasium, space for hosting varied events, a family enrichment center, and space for Jewish Family Service and the Solomon Schechter Day School. It was located on the same ten-acre plot purchased forty years earlier for the well elderly. The home for the latter had been opened in 1985.

The course of development that led to the creation of the community center was not without controversy. The religious side sometimes saw in the organized secular arm a threat to its own hegemony and purpose. Rabbi Paul Citrin of Congregation Albert defined the problem in 1993 as one of survival, with the unique identity of the Jews at stake in an open society. He saw in the proposed center a false assumption, "that swimming and *schvitzing* [sweating] together guarantees Jewish survival somehow."[38] Survival for what purpose? he asked. "Have we made it for 3,500 years just to indulge in a certain amount of shallow, self-segregating togetherness?" His answer lay in having a higher purpose. The center, he contended, would draw funds away from synagogues and other community needs.[39] He did not win the argument.

The creation of a community center also attracted opposition from health club owners in the city. Some of them saw strong

FIGURE 5. Ronald Gardenswartz Jewish Community Center.
Courtesy of Ronald Gardenswartz Jewish Community Center.

competition in the nonprofit tax-exempt status that the new center would enjoy. Executive Director of the JFGA Andrew Lipman responded to the criticism by pointing out that the health and fitness facilities would be there as an adjunct to the widespread communal activities of the center. The sports and health facilities, he contended, were not there merely for their own sake. Lipman placed the agency in the same category as YMCAs.[40]

The dedicatory ceremonies for the new center reflected much that had occurred in the half century since World War II. The guests who spoke were a testament to the openness in which the community had flourished since the war. John Sandager of Hoffmantown Church and chair of Yad B'Yad (see chapter 6 on interfaith) spoke of it, while representatives from Laguna/Santo Domingo Pueblo, the National Hispanic Cultural Center, and the New Hope Church on behalf of the African American Christian community performed or made statements.[41] It was indeed a long step from the relatively narrow outreach of the two Albuquerque congregations that had existed at the end of the Second World War. Indeed, it announced in stone its mission of service to Jews and non-Jews. There was little in New Mexico at the moment that could surpass the optimism that the event promised.

Other noncongregational developments since World War II demand individual mention. The war years witnessed the creation of a chapter of Hadassah, an institution originally founded in 1912 to aid health standards in a then disease-ridden Palestine and bearing a strong Zionist concern. In New Mexico some of the leading personages who led the effort to organize were not of the old-line New Mexico families. Ilse Blaugrund, who had come

from Germany in 1938, and Shirley Gardenswartz, both of the original Hadassah group that had been formed in 1941, spoke of the
problem then of finding the necessary fifteen members required
to start the organization.[42] By the late nineties the Albuquerque
chapter claimed 514 members while the Santa Fe chapter had 143.
Other communities also formed Hadassah chapters. By the mid-
seventies Rio Rancho and Los Alamos women had followed suit.[43]
Las Cruces women also developed their own chapter. In late 1998
data showed 113 members at Los Alamos, 86 in Las Cruces, and
18 at Taos.[44] Clearly the organization was flourishing. Through
the varied mechanisms of speakers, style shows, rummage sales,
and luncheon meetings Hadassah met and even oversubscribed
its fund-raising goals.[45]

FIGURE 6. Professor Shlomo Karni,
editor of the *Link*. Courtesy of the *Link*.

Jewish Federation of Greater Albuquerque • 5520 Wyoming Blvd. N.E., Albuquerque, NM 87109
Dated Material • Return Service Requested

NON-PROFIT ORGN
U.S. POSTAGE
PAID
ALBUQUERQUE, NM
PERMIT NO. 492

New Mexico Jewish
the LINK

VOLUME 29, NUMBER 6

TAMUZ/ AV / AUGUST 2000

FIGURE 7. *Link* masthead. Courtesy of the *Link*.

Other visible and valuable new institutions also made an appearance. In 1971, Shlomo Karni, an engineering professor at the University of New Mexico, saw the need for a medium to relate community news and express community needs.[46] The AJWF concurred with Karni's views and early on paid the bills for publishing the Albuquerque community *Link*, a monthly printed bulletin. Professor Karni assumed the editorial functions of the journal until 1975 and stayed on as editor until that time.

In the late eighties, growth in circulation and the increasing expense involved in publication led the federation to introduce considerable changes. The *Link* had to become financially self-sufficient. To fulfill that requirement the paper needed to become a professional publication and to seek advertising to meet its costs. It also had to free itself of its perceived attachment to the Federation and return to its original focus as a community journal.[47]

By the year 2000 much of that change had been achieved. In 1990 its circulation had been 1,600. At its twenty-fifth anniversary in 1996 that number had risen to 3,400 with an additional 1,900 copies distributed to Jewish institutions, bookstores, and restaurants. In 2000 distribution had reached some 7,000 copies monthly. Advertising income rose from $3,000 in 1987, when

Judith Carr joined the staff, to $22,000 in 1988 and to $58,000 in 1996.[48] Professor Karni's original intent had achieved its purpose and the *New Mexico Jewish Link*, renamed in 1996, had become the most available and fullest source for knowledge of activities of the Jewish community in New Mexico.

Another sign of the increasing awareness of New Mexico's Jews of their environment came with the formal creation of the New Mexico Jewish Historical Society in 1985. Interest in such an organization dated back to the late 1970s. Scholarly publication about early Jewish settlers in the territory had appeared at least as early as 1960 in the work of William J. Parish, an economics professor at the University of New Mexico. Even earlier, his master's thesis at Harvard had examined the pioneer Ilfeld family business in Las Vegas.[49] Parish's choice of subject matter did not rest primarily on an interest in New Mexico's Jews per se. Nevertheless, his research and publication called attention to the early presence and economic character of Jews in New Mexico. It was not long before other historians, such as Rabbi Floyd Fierman of El Paso, devoted themselves to uncovering the presence of other Jewish families. Rabbi Fierman's publications indicated a clear interest in local Jewish history and attracted wide attention.[50]

It was the relative newcomers who took the lead in broadening and formalizing the historical interest in an institutional manner. A. David Scholder, who had not been in Santa Fe long, recorded the first formal event of the Historical Society—a program on the Jews of New Mexico—in August 1985. Despite the keen cultural competition of the city, 230 persons attended the event.[51] By late 1987 the organization counted over one hundred members.[52] In early 2000 the membership had grown to a robust three hundred.[53] Although concentrated in Santa Fe in its origins, and with over a third of its members still there, participation had extended to most major cities in the state and included no small number of out-of-state members.

The activities of the organization ranged over a broad spectrum. It collected historical materials and saw to their preservation. It produced annual programs featuring themes of Jewish history in New Mexico that included biographical information on past generations of Jewish settlers, the Jews at Los Alamos, the role of Jewish women, relations with Native Americans, and even the experiences of Jewish hippies in Taos. It also took upon itself the annual task of cleaning up the cemetery of the virtually defunct Jewish community of Las Vegas. By 2000 the society's activities had organized a regular agenda and expressed a deep and open consciousness of its interest and pride in the participation and achievements of the Jews in the territory and state.

In the late nineties the increased awareness of Jewish participation in the history of territorial New Mexico led to the creation of a special exhibition at the Palace of the Governors in Santa Fe on the lives and activities of Jewish pioneers in the nineteenth and early twentieth centuries. Conceived by Felix and Susan Warburg, she a descendant of the estimable Spiegelberg family of nineteenth-century Santa Fe, the enterprise attracted wide attention. It served as an impressive marker of increased Jewish participation not only for the successive generations of families who had settled in New Mexico but for the entire Jewish population and their desire and willingness to be recognized as a part of the region's history.[54]

The growth of the Jewish student population at the University of New Mexico led to the formalization of a Hillel group for Jewish students. Writing in 1972, Professor Gunther Rothenberg of the university's history department noted the sporadic existence of the group during the 1930s.[55] The matter of Hillel's existence is clear since the 1940s. In 1946 Lewis R. Sutin described the establishment of the councillorship, which he assumed at that time. Rabbi David Shor, who arrived in 1948, then took over those duties.[56]

Rothenberg's description spoke of some 400 Jewish students on the campus in the early seventies. He felt that the undeclared numbers might well be higher but the minutes of the Welfare Fund in 1970 found the number lower—at 250.[57] Hillel's facilities, however, consisted only of a mailbox and a social life of Sabbath celebrations at the homes of faculty members, with attendance bringing some thirty persons together.[58] Writing in 1987, Rabbi John Feldman, who became Hillel director in that year, praised both the Jewish Federation and B'nai B'rith for their financial support and the union of community and faculty representatives in efforts to bring stability to the organization.[59]

In 1993, Janet Gaines, in a report to the Jewish Federation and in her fifth year as Hillel's director, felt rather encouraged by its continued existence. Still getting turnouts of thirty to forty persons, she remarked on a visit by Lutherans who sought to learn how Hillel's attendance was so large as compared to their own when their numbers on campus and their facilities were so much larger than that of the Jewish student population.[60] Nevertheless, for those who regarded the numbers involved as small, the answer resided in the nature of campus life with its temporary population, its diversity, and the new freedom that university life spelled for many of the students.

In 1995 Hillel on the university campus reached a new level of good fortune. Paula Amar and Mel Schwartz donated a house to the organization in memory of their late son. In addition to traditional services, members found each other and opportunities to travel. Given the varied nature of campus life, Hillel members developed initiatives to overcome barriers with non-Jewish students, such as seeking to improve relations with Arab students through a Jewish/ Muslim dialogue. In 2001 there were an estimated 500 Jews on campus and 130 were active in Hillel.[61] The organization appeared to be flourishing at the turn of the century.

The activity of the Anti-Defamation League of B'nai B'rith (ADL) expanded in the postwar decades. Created to deal with anti-Semitism in 1913, its role in New Mexico grew as the state's isolation ebbed and national and international issues became an increasingly important part of its concern. Though anti-Semitism remained at the core of the ADL's concerns, new features emerged dealing with the range of issues surrounding civil rights. The new professional face of the Jewish community showed itself, attorneys often playing a role in the organization's activities. In the sixties, such persons as Milton Seligman and Michael Sutin—the first a descendant of an old New Mexico family, the second a new (postwar) family—assumed leadership roles in the organization. They reflected the new, more activist attitude of the Jewish community.[62]

Until 1990 the New Mexico ADL operated as a satellite under the regional administration of the Denver office. In that year, the ADL opened its own offices in New Mexico. Susan Seligman of Albuquerque served as state coordinator until 1992. At that time

New Mexico became a separate entity, having developed its own board and programs throughout the state. Richard Nodel became state chairman while Susan Seligman became a regional director.[63]

The nature of the times also led to the creation of special organizations. One of these unique groups was Cafe Europa. It was composed of persons who had escaped Nazism or the concentration camps. Their experiences gave them a bond that separated them psychologically from American-born Jews. The impetus for their togetherness appeared after the visit to New Mexico of the Anne Frank in the World Exhibit in 1995. Given the limited nature of their union, the organization could only have a future of decline.[64] Nevertheless, it was a heartwarming expression that eased the pain of their tortured past for its members. Another related organization, even though created just after the beginning of the twenty-first century, was the New Mexico Holocaust and Intolerance Museum, fostered by survivor Werner Gellert. At the time of writing it continues to function as a powerful reminder of the postwar mood of the Jews and a broader reminder of man's inhumanity to man that its creation sought to foster.

Santa Fe, too, moved to create a secular communal organization as its Jewish population expanded in the latter decades of the twentieth century. The Lebanese-Israeli war of the early eighties spurred concerned Jews to move beyond congregational organization to explain the Israeli position to non-Jews and to deal with anti-Jewish or anti-Israeli feelings. These circumstances led to the formation of a Jewish Community Council including Beth Shalom, B'nai B'rith, Hadassah, and the UJA. The Santa Feans looked to Albuquerque for guidance in early 1984 and established themselves formally as a council in that year.[65]

While the Jewish nonreligious organizational complex grew at a rapid pace in the postwar period, it was in many respects a replica of what was occurring to Jews nationally. The culture of organization spelled a change in how a considerable segment of New Mexico's Jews related to their ancestral culture. While congregational growth was great as population grew, the new extension of noncongregational growth defined an additional dimension of identification and participation enabled by the new numbers, energy, and support of the broad Jewish population.

The growth of an organized secular arm in New Mexican Jewry is certainly one of the important changes differentiating the postwar from the prewar Jewish community. The postwar period witnessed a considerable evolution of emphasis in its half century. Starting with an overwhelming concern for the welfare of refugees and the fate of Israel in the early decades after the war, that portion of the budget devoted to overseas concerns, although still large, gradually declined over time. The partial resolution of the problems abroad allowed that evolution. Israel faced continuing dangers but no full-fledged war between 1973 and 2000 and the immediate refugee problems incurred by World War II abated. Yet the potential for reoccurrence did not disappear, and new refugee problems appeared with the fate of the remaining Jewish population in the Soviet Union at stake. All in all, the concern with these issues outside of the United States still dictated that such problems receive the largest single item in the budget of the secular organization.

The last decades of the century witnessed increasing concern with the internal problems of New Mexican Jewry as its numbers grew and as those interests moved beyond the capacity of the congregations and of individual families to deal with them. In effect, they bear witness to a maturation induced by numerical growth and increased complexity as New Mexican Jewry acquired everbroader dimensions approximating the fullness of Jewish life in the United States.

CHAPTER FIVE

Congregational Growth
and Religious Change

*I*n 1940 a New Mexico Historical Records Survey prepared a "Directory of Churches and Religious Organizations in New Mexico." Evidence of three Jewish congregations reached the directory's researchers: Congregation Montefiore, founded in 1884 in Las Vegas but essentially dormant by 1940; Congregation Albert, founded in 1897 in Albuquerque; and Congregation B'nai Israel, also in Albuquerque, formally organized in 1920 and, unlike the other two Reform institutions, begun with Orthodox intent and gradually turned Conservative as a result of its inability to fulfill the requirements of Orthodoxy.[1]

Even the simplest comparison of 1940 congregations with those of the year 2000, using the regularly listed religious organizations in the *Link* at the latter date, displays a growth in their number and variety that would have been inconceivable in 1940. Notices for Albuquerque and vicinity alone carried seven listings, Santa Fe had six, and the rest of New Mexico listed nine more— a total of twenty-two.[2] In addition to their urban concentration there was also widespread geographic dispersion. The prewar Jewish merchants had established themselves in every well-populated place and even in many quite thinly peopled locales, only seemingly absent in the northwest corner of the state. It is the growth of urban congregations, however, and the variety of their religious expression that bespeak the major changes that have occurred since World War II.

In 1945 Congregation Albert of Albuquerque had been in existence for nearly a half century. It was, without doubt, the oldest functioning Jewish congregation in the state and, despite the difficulties it encountered during the Depression, offered a stable membership,

FIGURE 8. Congregation Albert. Courtesy of Israel C. Carmel Archive.

facilities, and a ministerial presence that allowed it to be identified as New Mexico's premier Jewish institution. This position appeared with particular sharpness in the early postwar years when Jewish numbers began to increase rapidly while the institutional base available to serve them grew at a relatively slow pace.

In part, Congregation Albert's primacy can be measured by the use made of it by Jewish organizations. Up to the early 1940s, B'nai Israel, by comparison, had no permanent location. To accommodate its growth, Congregation Albert built a new temple, its second, in 1950. For a time its facilities enabled it to host the variety of organizations that had existed earlier or were making an appearance— AJWF, youth groups, Hillel, Council of Jewish Women, and the older B'nai B'rith among them.[3] Its continuing growth led to the construction of yet another temple in 1984, still in use at the time of writing.

The congregation proved especially fortunate in its choice of leaders. The thirty-year career of Rabbi David Shor, from 1948 to 1978, remains unmatched in longevity by any other ministerial career in the history of New Mexico's Jews. And the congregation became aware of its good fortune early. By 1956 the members eliminated the clause from its constitution calling for a biennial election of a rabbi in favor of awarding him a lifetime contract.[4] The city of Albuquerque, too, showed its appreciation of him on the twenty-fifth anniversary of his rabbinate in 1973 by proclaiming a Rabbi Shor Day.

Upon Rabbi Shor's retirement in 1978, the congregation turned to Rabbi Paul J. Citrin as his successor. The choice again proved fortunate and his tenure lasted until 1996, when he chose to leave Albuquerque. He proved a strong activist in the stormy issues that

FIGURE 9. Rabbi David Shor.
Courtesy of Israel C. Carmel Archive, Congregation Albert.

arose in the eighties and nineties.[5] That only two rabbis led the congregation for forty-eight years was a testament to the stability of the congregation, and their leadership left a mark for the institution and for the Jews of Albuquerque. Rabbi Joseph R. Black, who succeeded Rabbi Citrin, appeared headed for another successful career in the year 2000.

The stability and growth of Congregation Albert provides the historian with an excellent perspective by which to measure the religious growth of New Mexico Jewry over the half century that has passed since World War II. Using membership increase as a measuring stick, the congregation offers a picture of steady growth, particularly when observed by decades. In 1944 there were 87 congregants and in 2000, 626 families.[6] That was nearly an eightfold increase. As with many New Mexico statistics, however, the rate of membership growth was most rapid in the period between 1950 and 1970, when it doubled. Other overlapping twenty-year periods show a similar rate of growth, with the slowest increase between 1980 and 2000. Even so, a growth rate of nearly 80 percent in that last generation demonstrates a healthy increase.

In addition to its fortunate choices of rabbinical leadership, the congregation enjoyed the healthy support of lay volunteers. Some of them carried over from the prewar years. The name of Max N. Fleischer as secretary appears from the early 1930s to the mid-1950s with little interruption. Family generational participation also leaps off the listings. Members of the Seligman family of Bernalillo recur as congregation presidents from the early thirties to 1960. The pattern changes slowly in the postwar period, with less repetition of names, possibly as a result of the availability of so many new and willing members.[7]

FIGURE 10. Rabbi Paul Citrin. Courtesy of the *Link*.

Congregation B'nai Israel's experience in the early decades after the war also showed an estimable path of growth, although somewhat slower than Congregation Albert's. With 60 members in 1941, the number rose to 195 in 1955. By 1980 it had expanded to 410. Henceforth, growth came more slowly. In 1995 the congregation's numbers had risen only to 485. By the year 2000, however, membership had suffered a decline to 383.[8] Nevertheless, the growth of B'nai Israel for the entire postwar period was still over sixfold.

B'nai Israel could point with pride to the course of its postwar development. The congregation had to build a new synagogue in 1970 to accommodate its growth. And, like Congregation Albert, it found an estimable leader in Rabbi Isaac Celnik, who in 1997

FIGURE 11. Temple B'nai Israel. Courtesy of Stephanie Spinks.

FIGURE 12. Rabbi Isaac Celnik. Courtesy of the *Link*.

celebrated twenty-five years at his post. He received the plaudits of the entire city when Mayor Martin Chavez proclaimed January 11 as Rabbi Isaac Celnik Day in Albuquerque.

The distinctly different course of growth presented by the last generation at B'nai Israel is a matter of interest and conjecture. The last years of the century, when the actual decline in membership took place, appears to have been the result of internal congregational matters that produced discomfort for some. Such matters extend beyond the range of a general history of the Jewish population and belong to a future history of the congregation itself. However, some characteristics of B'nai Israel's historical path are clear. In 1980 about 20 percent of its membership was made up of retirees. By the year 2000 that figure had risen to 36 percent. Thus aging and death may account partially for the slowed growth.

One of the great changes in congregational development in the postwar era lies in the expansion of variety of religious expression. Less traditional congregational forms reflecting postwar trends among American Jewry made an appearance. In Albuquerque, the formation of Congregation Nahalat Shalom (Inheritance of Peace) in 1983 is an example. Its originator, Rabbi Lynn Gottlieb, arrived with some claim to national visibility as an already established female rabbi. Acquainted with New Mexico through family ties, she found her way to residence in Albuquerque through an invitation to participate in the Experiment in Jewish Living in 1982. As one of a handful of female rabbis in the country, she combined her powerful Jewish feminist impulse and democratic activism with mysticism and strong artistic expression to seek a reconstructed Judaism. Formally, she described the congregation as Renewal/Independent.

Her openness to intermarried couples, gay parishioners, and single-parent households found resonance among Jewish New Mexicans who often lived beyond the bounds of traditional Jewish social life.[9] Accepting of these less than traditional forms, Rabbi Gottlieb's personality itself exercised a strong hold on her followers.

The congregation was composed mostly of persons new to New Mexico, many of whom had never before affiliated with formally organized Judaism. The membership has been described as one of artists, professionals, public servants, mixed-faith families, same-sex households, and single-parent homes.[10] They may have felt more comfortable under Rabbi Gottlieb's welcoming umbrella than in more traditional congregational settings.

The course of Rabbi Gottlieb's career did not always proceed smoothly. Her private ordination as a rabbi was an early source of mistrust among an older Jewish population. Her gender was also not immediately accepted as appropriate for a rabbi among some in the Jewish community. With the passage of time, however, some of these differences with other local clerics abated.[11] She also played an active role in the issue of the Palestinian-Israeli conflict, reaching out to Arab Americans, "trying to create an atmosphere of hope."[12] However, some of her positions on Israeli-Palestinian relations—critical of Israel—brought about a longer lasting enmity with segments of the Jewish community.[13]

Nevertheless, her congregation grew well. In 1987 it claimed more than 50 households and in 1997 a membership of more than 130 households.[14] In the year 2000, that number had risen to 180 households. In the latter year the congregation found the means to establish a home for itself after "schlepping [dragging] from house to house," as Rabbi Gottlieb put it.[15]

FIGURE 13. Rabbi Lynn Gottlieb. Courtesy of the *Link*.

By the early 1970s the institutionalization of congregations dissatisfied some of the postwar newcomers to Albuquerque. Their response was to create a new, yet old, form of community called *chavurah* (fellowship), which had emerged on the American Jewish religious scene during the early 1960s. The originators and early members of the group were largely employed at either Sandia

Corporation or the University of New Mexico. Stressing individual bonds of friendship and family and seeking to educate themselves in matters of Judaism, these largely Conservative and relatively young believers formed Chavurat Hamidbar (Fellowship of the Desert) in 1973, celebrating holidays in members' homes without formal rabbinical leadership.[16]

Often highly educated and secure in their capacity to fend for themselves, the chavurah grew well. They educated their children at their Hebrew school, which counted twenty pupils in 1974. Until the 1980s their numbers remained small—thirty to thirty-five members—and retained the educational character with which the original six members had begun. By the late eighties the slowly aging membership experienced problems in the maintenance of their school, and they had to consider the issue of a cemetery for members. Nevertheless, the chavurah experienced continuing growth, some of it composed of persons who had left B'nai Israel, and in 2000 it consisted of about eighty-five families—a size that the membership still found compatible with their original intent.[17]

The constancy and growth of this congregation spoke to the expanding religious dimensions of New Mexico's Jewish population. It presented a picture of confidence and visibility that moved beyond any notion of safety in numbers. And although they began with a generally conservative—that is, a traditional—emphasis in their practice, in time they trusted themselves to adjust to such contemporary issues as the place of women in Judaism. The group accepted them as participants in services in an egalitarian spirit.[18] In effect, the congregation bespoke the broadening of perspective and organization that has proven to be an important characteristic of post–World War II Judaism in New Mexico. It was not a product of radicalism or charisma, but an extension of traditional form within mainstream American Judaism.

In the early 1990s the broadening spectrum of Jewish religious identification added another new presence with the arrival of Rabbi Chaim Schmuckler. He had served as a chaplain at Philmont Boy Scout Camp near Cimarron for two summers, became acquainted with Albuquerque, and decided in 1992 to start a Chabad (House of Worship) center there upon learning of interest among local Jews. By 1994 the Chabad had moved from the rabbi's rooms to a building on San Pedro just south of Montgomery.

Rabbi Schmuckler's Judaism was rooted in Hasidism, a movement that had begun in the western regions of the Russian Empire in the second half of the eighteenth century. Early on, mass enthusiasm, ecstasy, close group cohesion, and charismatic leadership were its distinguishing socioreligious characteristics.[19] Hasidism grew out of the Orthodox branch of Judaism, but as its adherents moved westward into the United States during the mass migrations from Eastern Europe between 1880 and 1924, its character diluted somewhat.

Quite distinct from the Reform assimilatory tradition of western Europe, the Hasidim sought to follow the letter of Jewish law and customs and even retained at times the distinctive dress of the East European shtetl (small town) with the long black coat, black hat, and beard of their forefathers. Rabbi Schmuckler dons his traditional clothes only on the Sabbath and holy days.[20] In July 1998 Chabad even opened a *mikvah*, a ritual bath for women, as part of its facilities and the only one in Albuquerque at the time.

Although Santa Fe was the first town inhabited by Jews in the new territory of New Mexico, just before the mid-nineteenth century, it would be more than a full century before a formal Jewish congregation would make an appearance in the city. It took Albuquerque and Las Vegas less than half that time. However, it should be noted even early Protestants were relatively slow in developing formal religious institutions in Santa Fe.[21] The answer may lie in the presence of a powerful Catholic church, the city's political position as capital of the territory, and the character of the early Jews and Christians who came there. A chapter of B'nai B'rith was organized in 1936 in the city—over a half century after Albuquerque did so, but by that time a new Jewish population had arrived in Santa Fe.

The leisurely pace toward religious organization was probably hastened by the events of World War II and its immediate aftermath. The shadow of Los Alamos, built to create the atomic bomb, hung over Santa Fe. The new research center attracted Jewish scientists in some numbers, and Santa Fe, the closest large town, served some of them as an urban center. Additionally, during the war the town also became the site of the Bruns Army General Hospital, where wounded Jewish soldiers were among those recuperating. A Jewish resident of the early postwar days noted that these newcomers "were astonished to find no temple or community to accommodate them. . . . [Being] Jewish took on a new significance."[22]

The chronology of change, while not electrifying, was nevertheless quite steady, considering the small number of persons involved. In late 1946, a meeting called under the auspices of B'nai B'rith created an entity called the Santa Fe Jewish Temple. It was incorporated shortly thereafter. The well-known Pick brothers, Marcel and Emil; Julius Gans; Daniel Taichert; Marcia Hertzmark;

FIGURE 14. Santa Fe activist Leah Kellogg. Courtesy of the *Link*.

Louis Rubenstein; and Albert Kahn were among its incorporators. They purchased a site on Barcelona Road and in 1949 changed the name to the Santa Fe Jewish Temple and Community Center, Inc. Twenty-four persons attended the meeting at which the name change took place.

Plans for a building were drawn in the early fifties and the task awarded to John Gaw Meem, a noted New Mexico architect intimately associated with the creation of the Santa Fe style of architecture. The official dedication took place on June 2, 1956. At that time the temple had fifty members in good standing, and a search for a rabbi ensued.[23] In the late fifties, Rabbi Abraham Shinedling of Albuquerque, a so-called "pinch-hit" pastor for the various roles he fulfilled in New Mexico and his love of baseball, became a part-time rabbi of the congregation and remained so for many years, with periodic interruptions when full-time rabbis took over.

Despite a growing Jewish population in the city, the congregation still had only 44 family members in 1968 out of 210 identified Jews in the city. In 1970 the congregation again changed its name to Temple Beth Shalom, which it still bore in the year 2000. The early seventies produced more dramatic changes. Events such as the murder of Israeli athletes in Munich, West Germany, in 1972 may have sparked an increased desire to affiliate more closely with Judaism, and between 1971 and 1974 the size of the congregation doubled to 85 families. The range of activities also expanded, giving rise "to a choir, a renewed Sisterhood, and a thriving religious school."[24]

By the seventies, too, the employment of full-time rabbis had become customary although the congregation could not always sustain it. In 1974 Rabbi Leonard Helman joined the congregation after a four-year stay by Rabbi Sam Markovitz. Helman became a fixture

FIGURE 15. Rabbi Leonard Helman, Santa Fe.
Courtesy of Gail Rapoport.

who remained until 1991, while simultaneously serving as an attorney for the Public Service Commission. By that time the congregation had 285 family memberships. Rabbi Nahum Ward took over the post in 1993. Rapid growth continued throughout the nineties and the congregation directory for 2001 carried some 380 family and single memberships.

Beth Shalom had always carried the designation of the Reform branch of Judaism. Beginning in the 1980s, however, its premises began to serve as a home for the expanding religious dimensions of Santa Fe Jewry. Accordingly, the temple welcomed separate services for both Conservative and Orthodox prayer. The Orthodox community, under the name Kehillat Torah HaMidbar, which changed to Pardes Yisroel in 1991, operated the only full-time Hebrew Day School in New Mexico, with eight grades.[25] In 1997 Santa Fe was further colonized by a Chabad presence, following the earlier creation of the center in Albuquerque.

In 1995 Santa Fe witnessed the creation of a second Reform congregation—Beit Tikva. The desire for a smaller group and more traditional prayer motivated a number of families from Beth Shalom to form a chavurah. Rabbi Helman had left the state by that time but appeared willing to return, and these families, older and accustomed to him, led to the formation of the new congregation. In 2000 the congregation was still meeting at a Lutheran Church that accommodated its needs.[26]

The religious condition of Santa Fe undoubtedly underwent a transformation in the post–World War II city in favor of religious observance, particularly from 1970 on. However, the rapid growth of Santa Fe Jewry raises the issue of whether congregational membership, despite its large increases, was keeping pace with the general growth of the city's Jewish population. In May 1985, at a board meeting of Beth Shalom, a list of some eight hundred Jewish families in Santa Fe was presented to see who among them might be persuaded to join.[27] At that time slightly over two hundred families belonged to the congregation.

Among the post-1980 changes, as in Albuquerque, Orthodoxy made its appearance. Small, but determined, in 1988, Rabbi Shlomo Goldberg joined the recently formed Torah HaMidbar and opened a school. With twelve families at that time, the congregation for many years resided on the premises of Beth Shalom.

The presence of Jewish families in Las Cruces was not new, dating back to the mid-nineteenth century. However, they had not created their own formal religious institution before World War II. As noted earlier, the *American Jewish Year Book* counted thirty-four Jews in 1940, one hundred in 1973, and six hundred in 2000. Before World War II and in the early postwar years, the city's proximity to El Paso, Texas, where congregation and rabbis existed earlier than in Las Cruces, provided some of the religious amenities that did not exist in Las Cruces before the war. Indeed, the record of the El Paso Jewish Federation in 1947 lists contributions from a number of leading Jewish citizens of Las Cruces, including a $1,500 check from L. E. Freudenthal, a descendant of one of the oldest Jewish families in that city.[28]

By 1953 the growing number of Jews allowed for an independent path. They created a religious school. In December of that year the first Chanukah celebration took place with one hundred guests in attendance from Las Cruces and the surrounding area.[29] In 1955 the adults organized a Las Cruces Jewish Community group that became a lasting body.[30] A more denominationally oriented formal organization, Temple Beth-El, came into existence in the 1960s. In 1967, Eugene Stern, an economically successful member of the community of long standing, gave well over half of the necessary sum toward the cost of the building that housed the congregation.[31]

As noted earlier, New Mexico's postwar population explosion included the development of totally new communities. Albuquerque's growth did not stop at the old boundaries of the city. West of the Rio Grande and to the north, at the end of the war, stood ranches that developers eagerly seized upon to meet the voracious demand for housing. In the early sixties, in what became one of the largest real estate developments in the United States, the American Realty and Petroleum Corporation (Amrep), purchased some 55,000 acres, later adding 37,000 more, and began to sell lots and to develop a town that took on the name of Rio Rancho.

In an ambitious advertising campaign that stretched across the country but with an early emphasis on the East Coast and the Midwest, Amrep advertised low-cost homes, excellent weather, and the nearby presence of Albuquerque as inducements to potential purchasers. At first, persons seeking affordable retirement locations formed a significant proportion of those who came. So successful was the venture that Rio Rancho became the fastest growing town in New Mexico by the mid-eighties, increasing its population from 1,300 in 1970 to 10,000 in 1980 and to more than 51,000 in 2000.[32]

Given the heavily northeastern emphasis of Amrep's early advertising, new Jewish residents arrived from that area who, in relatively short order, communed with each other. A study of religious institutional attendance found their numbers at 3 percent of the total population.[33] Some of the newcomers found the distance to the established Jewish congregations in Albuquerque inconvenient to travel. By 1974, sufficient numbers existed to form a Jewish social club, and a more formal Rio Rancho Jewish Center came into being in 1976. A meeting to discuss the creation of a synagogue in early that year drew some two hundred persons, although not all were locals. Through a variety of fund-raising devices, including bingo, the center purchased the Amrep building in 1978 and had paid off the mortgage by 1981. By the time of the formal mortgage-burning ceremony in 1982, fifty-five families belonged.[34]

In general, the new congregation leaned toward Conservatism. Although the group organized a sisterhood, a men's club, and even a Hebrew school, its ability to retain a rabbi was marginal over the years and educated laymen frequently undertook the task of religious leadership. In 1997, a knowledgeable layman, Aron Straser, assumed those duties.

Perhaps the most distinctive new town in postwar New Mexico was Los Alamos. It was established originally as a military post during the war with the express mission of developing the atomic bomb. It became a permanent facility and town after the war and remained a major research center. In its wake, it brought new industries to New Mexico that affected the entire economy of the state. Access to its premises was highly restricted until 1957, when it opened its gates to the outside world.

As noted earlier, Jewish scientists and engineers arrived from the earliest days of Los Alamos's existence. Some of the early senior scientists were Jewish refugees. During the war years sufficient numbers of Jewish personnel existed to hold gatherings whenever the frenetic work schedule permitted.[35] An information sheet distributed at the base listed announcements of services in the summer of 1944.[36]

When the war ended, steps toward more formal organization took place. In the summer of 1948 a B'nai B'rith Lodge was created with nearly one hundred persons attending its installation at the La Fonda Hotel in Santa Fe in August.[37] The women formed a chapter of Hadassah. In 1949 religious classes for young people began, and in 1954 a Jewish Center was organized. Some twenty families took on the responsibilities for it. The quest for a building began but was actualized only in 1964.

Given the variety of congregational loyalties among the Jewish personnel, the center did not affiliate with any specific branch of Judaism. In 1988 it advertised itself as a community of fifty-five families that held member-led services and assumed a middle-ground approach to Judaism for a population that ranged from Reform to moderate Orthodox. One could find such persons as Jack Schlachter—a rabbi and a physicist—who arrived in 1979 but did not serve formally as a rabbi for the community.[38] In 1988, however, the organized community was seeking a part-time rabbi who could provide educational guidance for its religious school and participate in adult educational activities.[39]

Even as new towns appeared in New Mexico with new Jewish populations, some older towns, where Jews had resided in the nineteenth century but had virtually disappeared as a result of changed economic conditions, began to reemerge as places of residence. Taos, which had attracted Anglo artists from the late eighteenth century and hippies in the 1960s, developed as a tourist attraction because of the remarkable pueblo that graced the town, the unspoiled beauty of the area, and the development of skiing facilities. Taos became a new center of organization among Jews who came to the area. They, like other seekers, were drawn to the small town for its quiet and beauty.

There had been a number of Jewish hippies in the late sixties and early seventies who had left middle-class Jewish life elsewhere to create a new existence removed from what they considered a too materialistic, artificial way of life. One of them, Iris Keltz, eventually found affinities between her original Judaism and the more basic lifestyle of New Buffalo, the hippie commune.[40] She and other later arrivals to the town also discovered similarities between the biblical ways of the Jews and those of the Pueblo Indians of the area. Despite her self-discovery, however, Keltz did not become a permanent resident and later moved to Albuquerque. Jews in this isolated northern New Mexico area also found traces of crypto-Judaism among the Hispanic population.

By the early 1980s the town dwellers contained enough Jews who had found each other to create a chavurah, B'nai Shalom, and even a cemetery. They met in members' homes and by the late nineties had created a religious school and hired rabbis for holidays.[41] In 1993 they formed the Taos Minyan (ten men) and in 1998 Jewish Renewal established a presence. In 2002 a sufficient number had shown interest to warrant the creation of a Taos Jewish Center. The "coming out" celebration drew one hundred Jews from the area. How many more lived in the vicinity is unknown, but locals estimated that the number could reach five hundred.[42] If that number was correct, it would appear that relatively few sought to associate themselves with their more openly Jewish brethren.

Las Vegas, which had created the earliest Jewish congregation (1884) in New Mexico, presented a unique case in which a thirty-year decline before World War II began to reverse itself in the late twentieth century. In the late nineties Marvin Taichert, then in his mid-sixties, described himself as "the only (Jewish) resident who was born here."[43] Taichert noted the influx of newcomers.

Strong signs of the past remained in the city, unlike the condition of the new towns or those where one family had been established. The old synagogue building had been sold to the Las Vegas Bible Church in the late 1950s by Milton Taichert, Marvin's father, but still existed. Some of the old houses showed evidence of where mezuzahs had once been attached to doorposts.[44] The old cemetery, too, still existed and began to receive annual cleanups through the efforts of the New Mexico Jewish Historical Society and the Las Vegas Montefiore Cemetery Committee, inspired by Taichert. The old Ilfeld Company building, one of the largest of the old Jewish family businesses, also still stood on the old plaza with its name emblazoned on its side.

By the turn of the twenty-first century it may be a matter of definition as to whether Las Vegas's Jewish community had reached the level of a congregation. Melanie LaBorwit, who assumed the post of Las Vegas Museum director in 1996, spoke of the warmth with which she was received by persons of crypto-Jewish ancestry and by descendants of intermarried settlers.[45] Attempts of Jews to meet regularly in the mid-nineties had faltered but not ceased. While the earliest generations of German Jewish settlers had much in common culturally and economically, the new influx was much more diverse.

In 1997 a Chanukah party drew one hundred attendees from the town and surrounding areas. Other Jewish holidays served as points of social gathering. Yet more formal commitments for such matters as education appeared to come only slowly. By 1999, however, a Jewish Community of Las Vegas had come into existence—at least a first step toward affiliation if not a formal congregation.

Like Taos, Carlsbad, in southeastern New Mexico, had a long history of a Jewish family presence. The notable Joseph and Herman Wertheim families were among them. However, their numbers were small, and the remoteness of the area from other urban centers never permitted any formal congregation to develop. Nevertheless, the High Holidays were celebrated without fail, and even non-Jewish clergy attended.[46] In 1998 the town was treated to its first bar mitzvah in thirty years. Mark Sanford, the honoree's father, believed that a slight majority of the guests were non-Jewish friends of the family.[47]

By the mid-nineties sufficient numbers of Jews and means of communication had grown up in surrounding areas that the beginnings of congregational life became possible. Computer networking and the existence of the *Link* aided the process of making Jews aware of each other's presence.[48] Long a tourist attraction noted for its famous caverns, the creation of the Waste Isolation Pilot Plant (WIPP) site for the burial of atomic waste materials broadened its employment base.

As early as 1988 newcomers to the area, joined by some long-term residents, had met monthly on Friday evenings and had services conducted by persons with some rabbinical education.[49] Mark Merrian, the president of the group, described its members as doctors, lawyers, engineers, and retirees with an average age of fifty. There were no children of Hebrew school age.[50] To him, both the small numbers and the demographic character of the participants did not seem to promise a bright future. Yet in 1996 a regional chavurah formed under the name of Mishkan Shalom with ties between Roswell, Ruidoso, Alamogordo, Hobbs, and Carlsbad. By 2002, about twenty families moved their services into the area's first synagogue. Its dedication even included an address by then gubernatorial candidate (and later governor) Bill Richardson. The development of the entire project was encouraged by the example of Taos.

The chavurah professed a Reconstructionist point of view and announced its adherence to Reform Judaism. Still in its early stage of development, it did not yet have a rabbi and hoped for a nuclear scientist at WIPP who might also be a rabbi. Aid—in the form of occasional use of rabbis from Las Cruces and the borrowing of a Torah from Roswell—supported the existence of the congregation.[51]

Roswell, in the southeastern quadrant of New Mexico, had long been a place of residence of Jews with an interest in maintaining their religious beliefs. A common meeting place had been the home of one of the most illustrious of early New Mexican Jews, Nathan Jaffa. Not only did he build a successful business and maintain his Jewishness, but he also had a distinguished political career, having been secretary of the territory for a number of years before statehood. Attempts among Jews to formalize themselves as a congregation had come as early as 1903.[52]

The town, which experienced recurrent economic difficulties, received a strong boost during World War II with the creation of

Walker Air Force Base about eight miles to its south. In 1949 the base became part of the Strategic Air Command. Jewish military personnel swelled numbers to a point where the spatial capacity of the church building used for services scarcely sufficed. It was during the early 1950s that Temple B'nai Israel was born, but never had a sufficient membership to employ a full-time rabbi.[53] Nevertheless, regular Friday night services and gatherings to celebrate Jewish holidays continued under the leadership of Daniel Lehman and Sam Stolaroff. Residents recall that Richard Tucker, the renowned operatic star, sang Kol Nidre at the Yom Kippur service in 1954.[54]

In 1967, however, the base was closed down. Despite the loss to the community, the supporters of a common religious presence remained. A reply to an inquiry from North Dakota by the secretary noted, "Our congregation is quite small. We have a synagogue but no rabbi. Services are conducted Friday evenings by members of the congregation and may be either conservative or reform. Kosher meat is not available." Florence Plaut, the secretary, spoke highly of the town's friendliness and the strong feeling of community among its Jews.[55]

In 1980 the congregation was formally incorporated with Seymour Beckerman as its president. In 1981 it counted "some twenty members."[56] By 1986 the city and surrounding area, in Beckerman's calculation, might have counted some one hundred Jews, although many did not formally associate with B'nai Israel. The congregation then consisted of about thirty members.[57]

By the turn of the twenty-first century, Roswell's economy again appeared to slow down. The Jewish population followed the path of the economy, with the number of congregation members falling to about twenty families, who stoutly maintained their loyalty. Newcomers were retirees and as a result children were gradually disappearing from among the membership. However, Jewish students at the New Mexico Military Institute—about ten a year—joined the older members.[58] The future bore a question mark although Roswell had recovered from the worst of its economic misfortune.

By late in the twentieth century New Mexico had become home for Jewish seekers of both old and new spirituality, as it had for persons dissatisfied with the general state of America in the sixties. If Rabbi Gottlieb portrayed elements of feminism as one facet of her approach to Judaism in the eighties, Rabbi Gershon Winkler in the nineties, trained as an Orthodox rabbi, felt that the limited atmosphere of that perspective demanded a broader spectrum of Jewish teaching to allow Jews "to have an easier way of relating to their heritage."[59] His odyssey took him to New Mexico in 1993.

Seeking his own path, he established himself near the small town of Cuba, where he created the Walking Stick Foundation. Like other new seekers, he found in Navajo rituals an earth-based interpretation of faith that he felt could have come out of Leviticus. His ministry defined itself as dedicated to "the restoration and preservation of aboriginal Jewish spirituality."[60] Retreats, rather than a formal congregation, became his vehicle to teach interested Jews of his views. Jewish shamanism frequently became the focus of their discussions. Indeed, the board of the foundation included Native Americans. In 1998, thirty persons attended the retreat, many of them Jews who had looked to Native American spirituality and now found similar sources in

FIGURE 16. Rabbi Gershon Winkler. Courtesy of the *Link*.

ancient Jewish spirituality.[61] New Mexico's Jews were acquiring the presence of a spectrum of religious expression that matched or even superseded the range available in much larger centers of Jewish population.

The post-eighties generation displayed a new process for religious organization. Earlier generations of Jews had sought each other out, communed with each other, and then combined to form a congregation. When they reached sufficient numbers they found a place to worship, and, lastly, sought a spiritual leader when they could afford it. The latest generation saw some reversal of that order. Such persons as Rabbis Schmuckler, Gottlieb, and Winkler did not come to congregations already formed as in the past, but as individuals who then drew congregants to themselves or had some awareness that they would be welcomed. Their followers were often persons dissatisfied with the practice of Judaism in the existing religious climate or persons who had ignored affiliation previously. In Winkler's case, he frequently served groups who did not live in New Mexico—often students from as far away as Berkeley. However, judging by the growth of the established congregations, the latter did not suffer greatly from the newcomers' appearance. The effect of the newcomers was to enlarge the spectrum of Jewish religious experience in New Mexico and to find points of accommodation with native religious traditions.

The study of kabbalah—"received tradition"—also made headway in the religious consciousness of New Mexicans in the last decades of the twentieth century. Although the phenomenon was national in its interest and included high-profile show business personalities, some New Mexico–based Jewish clergy saw in the openness of the southwestern landscape a special attracting point for the mystical dimension of kabbalah. All of the Jewish clergy saw virtue in its study although some felt that rational Judaism still represented its mainstream.[62]

Amid data on growth of congregations, the creation of new ones, and valiant attempts to recreate old ones, one is struck by the spirit and energy of many of the New Mexican Jews. Rabbi Leonard Helman, whose long career in Santa Fe led him to travel to Los Alamos and Taos as "outposts" of his activities, wrote in 1982 of a weekend in which he described some of his activities. They began with a Friday night service at his home base,

Congregation Beth Shalom. In brief, in addition to his sermon, the soloist sang a Yiddish song. On Saturday morning, a more traditional service was conducted by a local psychiatrist while another physician discussed the origins and meaning of women wearing the tallith.

On Sunday, Rabbi Helman drove to Los Alamos—a regular monthly feature of his activities. There he attended a conversion ceremony and a meeting at the Los Alamos Jewish Center at which the members discussed and committed themselves to an addition to the existing building. The rabbi also heard of attempts to develop a community at Taos.

Rabbi Helman ended his description of his experience thus: "At times I feel as if I were a rabbi with a congregation in Poland in the 11th or 12th century with Jews moving from Germany into a new frontier, or at times I sense what Jews experienced . . . in New York and in the Midwestern cities as they moved out of Europe, to build great Jewish centers. Northern New Mexico is in the great tradition of pioneer Jewish traditions, growing and developing spiritually and physically."[63]

A comparison of the state of religious organization in 1940 with that of the year 2000 reveals many of the changes that parallel other points of social development. The much larger population allowed new organizations to come into being without necessarily harming the older institutions. The greatly broadened social character of the new Jewish population supported the existing branches of Judaism that had grown out of the narrower ethnic character of the old population while allowing the creation of new ones. Even if unknown numbers of Jews did not affiliate with any formal groups, the continued presence and strength of the older institutions and the creation and variety of new ones suggest that a considerable increase of open religious expression and loyalty had grown up in New Mexico. Rabbi Helman's depiction easily applies to the rest of New Mexico. It presented a picture of maturation and optimism by the year 2000.

CHAPTER SIX

Interfaith Activity

$\mathcal{F}$or all Jews, the end of World War II brought an increased sense of urgency. The Holocaust and the creation and survival of Israel formed the central foci for their new concerns. A number of Christian churches also chose to reconsider their attitudes and relationship toward Jews as a result of these events. Out of these conditions a whole new dimension of interaction between Jews and Christians arose.

Anti-Semitism in New Mexico, however slight as compared with its European expressions or even those faced by Jews in the northeastern United States, was nevertheless present before the war. Aware of the existence of the age-old bias in the country as a whole, such organizations as the National Conference of Christians and Jews had been formed in 1927 by prominent laymen and clerics to promote understanding among differing faiths. The organization sponsored Brotherhood Days. One such commemoration took place in 1939 in Albuquerque. Additionally, prominent New Mexicans, clerics and laymen alike, supported appeals for international aid to Jews and other sufferers under the Nazis in the late thirties as their perilous conditions became increasingly evident and severe.[1] The major wartime and immediate postwar events affecting the Jews, however, radically altered the dimensions of how traditional religious institutions and persons regarded the historical relationship of Christian and Jew.

One cannot speak of anti-Semitism before the war without noting that there was also a history of generous cooperation between congregations of differing faiths in New Mexico. Time and again, dating back to the nineteenth century, the creation of new congregations without the resources to house themselves received support from established churches to use their facilities for prayer and meeting. That tradition was still in force at the turn of the twenty-first century.

The most dramatic postwar change came in Catholic-Jewish relations. The Catholic Church, partially as a result of the war, undertook a major effort to reexamine itself under the urging of Pope John XXIII. Through his efforts the Church convened an extraordinary meeting in the first half of the 1960s. That gathering has become known historically as Vatican II. Among the topics subjected to scrutiny was the Church's relationship to the Jews as well as to other religious faiths. At the end of the council's deliberations in 1965 it incorporated its views into a statement entitled *Nostra Aetate* (In Our Time). Concerned with promoting the unity of the human family, the document placed emphasis on common elements between religions as a basis for dialogue. Insofar as it dealt with Jews, the statement denied the blame for Christ's death on all Jews alive in his time as well as on contemporary Jews and decried anti-Semitism.[2] For the Church, this was a radical change with powerful implications as to how Catholics were to regard Jews and behave toward them.

The Church continued to expand those positions in the post–Vatican II decades. In 1975 the National Conference of Christian Bishops reiterated the condemnation of anti-Semitism and encouraged interreligious dialogue.[3] In 1998, examining the Church's behavior during the war, the bishops asked Jews for forgiveness for the sins of passivity they had displayed under the Nazis. Again, in 2002, a statement under the imprimatur of the U.S. Conference of Catholic Bishops included the declaration that "campaigns that target Jews for conversion to Christianity are no longer theologically acceptable in the Catholic Church."[4] The effects of such declarations served as incentives for the opening of a new era in Catholic-Jewish relations. Those changes of position were still playing themselves out in the early years of the twenty-first century.

The long history and dominating presence of Catholicism in New Mexico provided ample opportunity for the revised doctrines and attitudes to work themselves out in practice. Even before Vatican II, however, there was growing evidence that Catholic-Jewish relations were changing in favor of greater cooperation and understanding in the Mountain West. An Anti-Defamation League bulletin pointed out such a trend in 1961, and the Denver *Catholic Register* published an article to that effect in the same year, noting that it had begun in the Denver area over a year earlier.[5]

Many Protestant groups also made evident similar concerns and adopted actions to improve their relationship with Jews. Vatican II also affected Catholic relations with a broad spectrum of Christian groups. Although Protestants in New Mexico had begun to think in ecumenical terms shortly after World War II, it was in 1964 that they founded the New Mexico Council of Churches with a focus on cooperation in human services. In 1967 the Archdiocese of Santa Fe joined, the first diocese in the United States to enter an ecumenical council.[6] By the 1980s New Mexico's Jews were included in the council, and it had broadened the scope of its interests, advocating nonsectarian instruction in world religions in the public schools.[7]

New Mexico's Jewish religious institutions responded affirmatively to the new atmosphere. Rabbi David Shor, who assumed rabbinical duties at Congregation Albert in 1948, was a key figure in the early thought and actions toward greater religious understanding. A chaplain in the military during World War II, Shor believed that "the ecumenical movement started with the chaplains in the war."[8] A decade before Vatican II he was urging the Men's Club at Congregation Albert to invite rabbis to provide lectures for Albuquerque's Christian clergy and to help create an Institute on Judaism for Christian clergymen.[9]

Shor went well beyond a one-sided view in his efforts to improve understanding. In response to the ongoing work of Vatican II, the rabbi sermonized his congregation in 1963 with the question as to whether Jews should reevaluate their attitudes toward Jesus. He did not expect that they could accept him as the Messiah, but they could reassess their appreciation of him with an eye to improving their own understanding of Christianity.[10] Nor did the rabbi consider his suggestion as a quid pro quo for any steps that might be taken by Vatican II. The actions of the Ecumenical Council had to be recognized "as an act of historic justice . . . in and of itself."[11]

In his sermons the rabbi also laid emphasis on the commonly held beliefs of the two faiths and their mutual indebtedness to each other. He pointed to the Bible as "the most precious possession of both Christian and Jew." He then added, "Just as the knowledgeable Christian acknowledges his debt to Judaism for the Bible and for Jesus, so too, must the Jew acknowledge his debt to the Christian for the manner in which the knowledge of the Bible has been spread to all peoples everywhere. . . . .They have made it the world's most read and best loved book."[12] To him, it was a knot that tied the two faiths together.

And his actions proved his words. As early as 1969 the rabbi noted in a sermon that he was addressing as many as one hundred Christian groups a year—a major commitment on his part of time and energy.[13] He hammered the theme of respect for the beliefs and practices of others through understanding and learning and saw that respect as "the basic reason for the formation of dialogue groups."[14] By that time dialogue with Presbyterian groups had already begun to take place on a regular basis.[15] In 1972 Rabbi Shor even appeared as a cover photograph on the *Baptist New Mexican!*[16]

The congregations also moved beyond the historical religious boundaries of their faith. Through the creation of such organizations as the Temple Albert Men's Club (TAMC) in 1950, the members opened a path to a broad fellowship, Jewish and non-Jewish, of those interested in meeting (and eating, i.e., the cream cheese and lox factor) one Sunday a month to hear lectures and discuss subjects of common interest and concern. By 1975 the TAMC had 160 members and regarded itself as an "ecumenical club" open to all.[17]

In the seventies the Albuquerque rabbis reached out to their Christian counterparts to inform them about Judaism. Supported by a range of Jewish organizations, as well as the National Conference of Christians and Jews, they formalized a Judaic Institute for

Christian Clergy and brought in speakers to consider religious subjects of common interest.[18] In 1982, Reverend Ernest Falardeau of the Santa Fe Archdiocese and Rabbi Paul Citrin of Congregation Albert created what the Catholic clergyman defined as the beginning of a regular Jewish-Catholic Dialogue.[19]

The new open paths toward interreligious discussion also revealed new attitudes within the Jewish population. Although the Ashkenazic population had not hidden its existence in the prewar years, they had expressed themselves as Jews publicly with some modesty. These Jews had always participated in public affairs as citizens even though they had not stressed their Jewishness. The older historians of the prewar era, too, while including the role of prominent Jews in their works, laid no stress on their Jewishness. That, indeed, may have been their way of expressing tolerance.

The new issues confronting the Jews in the postwar era did not permit them the subdued expression of their religious identity that existed before the war. If one wanted to support Israel one's identity as a Jew involved the necessity of expressing oneself openly as a Jew and not merely as a citizen of New Mexico. If one felt deeply the condition of refugees in Europe that followed the Holocaust, expressing oneself as a Jew became a necessity in thought and action.

In the eighties, the pace of religious interaction quickened. A number of interactive events between Christians and Jews became annual affairs. In November 1980 Interfaith Thanksgiving services began, their location moving yearly. Starting in 1982, Holocaust Remembrance days involved a number of Jewish and Christian communities. In 1985, to mark twenty years since the end of Vatican II, Catholic and Jewish clergy exchanged visits at

FIGURE 17. Rabbi Isaac Celnik and Archbishop Michael J. Sheehan.
Courtesy of Cary Herz.

Yom Kippur and Mass—an unthinkable event for the previous history of both faiths.[20]

The first annual Jewish-Catholic Dialogue in New Mexico, cosponsored by the Archdiocese of Santa Fe, the Anti-Defamation League of B'nai B'rith, and the New Mexico Council of Churches, took place in 1994. The event took place in Albuquerque and in 1995 had spread to Santa Fe, where over one thousand persons attended the gathering.[21] In 1997 Santa Fe hosted its own Jewish-Christian Dialogue with addresses by a Jewish professor from the University of Notre Dame and a nun teaching at a Protestant seminary. The event was sponsored by the Ministerial Alliance of Santa Fe, the Archdiocese of Santa Fe, the New Mexico Council of Churches, Temple Beth Shalom, and the Anti-Defamation League.[22]

In the year 2000, remarkably, as it seemed to Albuquerque's leading rabbis, Archbishop Michael J. Sheehan spoke from the pulpit at Congregation B'nai Israel during the Sabbath service. The archbishop found the relationship in Albuquerque far in advance of other American communities and "rare" in the United States.[23]

The signs of interest and desire for interaction broadened steadily in the postwar years. In Albuquerque, some indigenous Evangelical Christians, who had believed in the rebirth of an Israel after the Jews accepted Jesus as the Messiah, had to deal with the reality of an existing Jewish state after 1948 without the Jews having accepted Jesus. Out of their religious interest and sympathy, and even without their prior knowledge of Vatican II, some sought to support the Jewish state through donations. They worked through Hadassah initially. In time, indeed, some joined Hadassah! In the mid-nineties they formed a group calling themselves Yad B'Yad

(Hand in Hand) to learn about Judaism and to support Israel. In 1996 Yad B'Yad had about eighty-five participants, a few of them Jews, who met monthly. Although the focus of the group was Israel, their studies took them into the Jewish roots of Christianity and the existence of anti-Semitism. As with New Mexico's Catholic Church, personal contact and discussion reduced age-old religious distance between some members of the two religions. One of the founders of the group in Albuquerque, Susan Sandager, even became involved in supporting the creation of similar groups in San Francisco, Fort Worth, and Houston.[24]

Santa Fe Christians created their own chapter of the organization.[25] Some Evangelical Christians expressed their support for the United Jewish Appeal's Operation Exodus, a campaign dedicated to the resettlement of Jews from Russia to Israel. Telethons over Santa Fe TV station KCHF, owned by Belarmino R. "Blackie" Gonzales, raised thousands of dollars for that purpose in 1994.[26] A remarkable step for interaction, albeit small, had occurred in New Mexico.

The course of interfaith activity after World War II was, however, not always in one direction. Although the event did not occur in New Mexico, the assertion by the president of the national Southern Baptist Convention in October 1980 that God did not hear the prayers of Jews set Jewish teeth on edge. Rabbi Isaac Celnik of B'nai Israel responded in the Albuquerque press that he did so because silence was not in order and displayed lack of respect for the faith of others. Reassertions of that doctrine at Southern Baptist Conventions occurred in 1996, accompanied by the belief of a need to evangelize Jews, a view expressed since the mid-nineteenth century.[27]

Such views left Jews with the age-old suspicion of the motives of non-Jewish religious organizations that sought to befriend them. Hadassah President Michaela Karni noted that when originally approached by Susan Sandager of Yad B'Yad with unsolicited financial support for Israel, she felt that "We still had our antennas up, like 'you want to convert us, right?'"[28] If anti-Semitism did not dispel quickly, neither did Jewish reactions to age-old attempts to proselytize them. Even after years of cooperation, Yad B'Yad's newsletter in March 2000, carrying its statement of purpose, offered a sensitive but necessary disclaimer to its readers that "This organization must not be a vehicle for any activity that could be interpreted as proselytizing, but rather a hand extended to our Jewish neighbors (both here and in Israel) in deep apology, promised support, and love that does not require anything in return."[29] Trust had to be learned despite the new climate that had emerged. Thus, although elements of older attitudes continued to exist, a new page had been written in Christian-Jewish relations, the course of which was still playing itself out in 2000.

Nor did the new spirit of interfaith discussion eradicate differences. Some Christian and Jewish positions on such issues as abortion continued to exist. However, the fact that persons in the two faiths could discuss them and still remain engaged with one another was part of the new attitude of respect that had emerged.[30]

Relations between American Indians and Jews also underwent a significant change. Individual contacts were a matter of long standing in New Mexico. They existed in the nineteenth century in the form of Jewish traders who dealt with the Native Americans. The most famous case of personal interaction came in the mid-1880s when Solomon Bibo, a trader, married a member of Acoma Pueblo and was chosen as its governor by the tribe. However, it was a century later that Jews and Native Americans began to encounter each other on an institutional ethno-religious basis rather than a purely individual one, allowing each group to look beyond the purely economic relationship of an earlier day.

One of the new threads of contact lay in Rabbi Gershon Winkler's vision of similarity between the Native Americans and Jews, which ushered in a dimension of contact undreamed of earlier. His Walking Stick Foundation, founded in the nineties with the Navajo tribe, was not a "congregation" in the usual sense but an avenue of mutual learning that addressed points of similarity without either group giving up its beliefs. At the turn of the century the enterprise was flourishing.

Contacts with other Native American tribes also arose in the late eighties. Group relations in the form of dialogues—that postwar instrument of interreligious discussion—came into existence with the aim of addressing issues of cultural survival, religious freedom, and the creation of an atmosphere of understanding where stereotypes had existed before. A formal Native American–Jewish Dialogue came into existence in 1989 with funding through the New Mexico Endowment for the Humanities.[31]

In the early nineties Anti-Defamation League officials and members of the Santa Ana Pueblo began meeting with each other. The intent was to learn and find common ground. In 1995, after learning that New Mexico's ADL was experiencing some financial difficulty, the pueblo presented the organization with a check. Roy Montana, the pueblo's leader, described the relationship between the two groups in moving terms: "Your history is our history."[32] The relationship had moved beyond the bounds of religion to include interethnic understanding. Perhaps it was an intertribal context.

Organized interfaith activity became an important new facet and fact of life for the Jewish people after World War II. Where ties of business and civic life had provided the major contacts between Jews and non-Jews before the war, common religious interest joined the older forms of contact as never before. And the tempo and strength of the contacts grew increasingly in the successive postwar decades. The growth of self-knowledge and awareness of historical and ethnic ties between the religious communities in the state must be considered one of the major new developments of the New Mexico religious scene. As with so many other areas of postwar development in New Mexico, the picture presented was heartwarming and optimistic. Indeed, of all the considerable changes that took place, the growth of interfaith activity stands out as the most original. What will happen subsequently belongs to the behavior and scrutiny of future generations and historians.

CHAPTER SEVEN

Issues

*J*ews almost everywhere have faced problems throughout their history based on the fact of their religious distinction and small numbers. These factors have shaped the legal, economic, and social character of their lives. Their experience in the United States voided any legal disabilities but left them with a social distinctiveness. World War II raised their consciousness as to both the dangers and the hopes of their condition.

A comparison between the two eras—prewar and postwar—in New Mexico reveals some differences. The state's relatively isolated character before the war changed after the war as a result of rapid growth, more varied social character, and the presence of a new economy. For the Jews of New Mexico, as noted throughout our examination, the expansion of economic and social diversity brought a broadened range of religious practice, and a felt need to respond openly to the major new problems—the aftermath of the Holocaust and the formation of the state of Israel—that intimately concerned them. The result produced a new dynamism in the search for answers to the new conditions. New Mexican history added its own unique issues to which its Jews responded. In some instances the issues existed within the community itself and solutions had to be found within it.

Anti-Jewish feeling, anti-Semitism, is historically the most painful and most widespread group experience encountered by Jews in Christian society. New Mexico, with its traditionally Catholic culture among Hispanos and its more recently introduced Protestant culture, in the presence of which the Jews were a tiny minority, could scarcely escape its existence. Yet, compared to the experiences of Jews elsewhere before World War II, in New Mexico its overt expression was slight. Anecdotal evidence offered by prewar Jewish settlers has always suggested a near absence of its existence and importance. Written evidence in business affairs indicates that it did exist but that it was quite minor compared to its European and even to its northeastern American expression before World War II. That viewpoint carried over into the postwar environment, and anti-Semitism's intensity was low compared to what the newcomers knew in their earlier environment. A visiting professor at the University of New Mexico expressed this view in *Harper's* in 1965. "I discovered," he wrote, "that there was virtually no anti-Semitism in Albuquerque."[1]

Despite such protestations, anti-Semitism did exist. The influx of new populations in the post–World War II period brought with it those attitudes that existed in other parts of the United States. Always sensitive to its presence, the events of the war and the postwar period increased the defensive reactions of New Mexico's Jews. However great the attestations of memoirs and interviews to its absence, anti-Semitism manifested itself in individuals, in organizations, and in acts that belie the denials of its existence. For instance, the creation of Israel brought not only a great upsurge of Jewish activity on behalf of the new state but also the existence of anti-Israel views. The influx of Arab students to American universities, for example, allowed their campus organizations to practice both anti-Israeli and anti-Semitic messages. The Cold War offered opportunities to those who viewed Jews as Communists—an old viewpoint, often when they backed civil rights causes—to disseminate their message. The range of messages afforded the anti-Semite grew even as did the messages of toleration and anti-discrimination.

The Anti-Defamation League (ADL), the Jews' chief institutional instrument to combat anti-Semitism, monitored its manifestations in individuals, organizations, and institutions where such a danger came to light. It noted the appearance of George Lincoln Rockwell, the leader of the American Nazi Party who spoke at Highlands University at Las Vegas. It posted notice of discriminatory content toward housing, incidents involving slights at hotels, and organizations where membership might be denied. Such activity was heavy in the 1960s when civil rights legislation became the law of the land.[2] Yet, in the view of Milton Seligman, an attorney and head of the ADL and a native New Mexican who lived in Albuquerque in the sixties, "Albuquerque was not a scene of big problems in anti-defamation at that time after the war. . . . We didn't have any real forceful bigots."[3]

There were, however, incidents worthy of note. One of the most dramatic, if short-lived, expressions of anti-Semitism since World War II in New Mexico was associated with the name of Reies Tijerina, a Hispanic figure of northern New Mexico who reached a considerable degree of popularity and notoriety in the second half of the 1960s. He sought redress of grievances that centered on land grant losses suffered by the "Indo-Hispano" population and discrimination against Spanish-speaking citizens. Tijerina identified Anglos and Jews as guilty of such behavior. He even quite mistakenly identified Thomas Catron, a most successful gatherer of land titles in the later decades of the nineteenth and early twentieth centuries, as a Jew.[4] External expression of such commentary faded when his short-lived political voice lost its public force.

Another painful episode occurred in the early 1980s involving the use of the name *Swastika* for the student yearbook at New Mexico State University in Las Cruces. An attempt by the ADL to end use of the name in the seventies failed. In 1983 a renewed attempt by the editor of the college newspaper, a Jewish student, brought out a heated reaction of views, both pro and con. The spectrum of opinion ranged from claims of insensitivity toward Jews and harm to the university on one end to criticism of Israel's treatment of Palestinians and Jews feeling sorry for themselves, to the defense of the symbol's use on the grounds of students' rights, its ancient use as a symbol by Native Americans, and the thought that no one cared about what happened fifty years ago. One adherent of changing the name commented, "You can't tell me that whenever you see a swastika painted on a wall that the first thing you think of is 'Go Aggies.'" There can be little doubt that an element of anti-Semitism existed in the controversy for some, but not all. The issue was hotly contested within the university and town and a balloting of students resulted in a majority for retention of the name. Governor Anaya, however, called for the end of its use and the Board of Regents complied.[5] The event produced pain for a time.

Nevertheless, despite these better known incidents, the over-all level of overt anti-Semitism in New Mexico remained low. For the most part, such open behavior occurred in the form of graffiti painted on visible Jewish institutions. An ADL report on anti-Semitic vandalism published in 1960, however, placed New Mexico in the lowest category of the occurrence of such events with one incident noted. The neighboring states of Arizona and Colorado had more examples than expected by correlation with state population. New Mexico did not even appear in the rankings.[6]

Spokespersons for the Jewish community at times were cautious in their interpretation of the meaning of such desecrations. When swastikas were painted on the doors of Congregation B'nai Israel in 1982, Rabbi Isaac Celnik thoughtfully recalled that after his initial shock, he feared an overreaction. He stressed the isolated character of the incident, the fact that churches too had been vandalized, and that a general insecurity prevailed in the entire society.[7] Similarly, the vandalizing of the Congregation Albert's cemetery in 1994 drew the opinion that Fairview Cemetery periodically served as a target for such behavior. ADL director Susan Seligman, by contrast, favored the view that it was an anti-Semitic act but attributed it to local gangs, weakening somewhat its specific intensity as an anti-Jewish target.[8]

Statistics on such incidents received much readier publicity in more recent decades than in the early years after the war. Most pronounced in the open battle against anti-Semitism was the activity of the ADL. Created in 1913 under the auspices of B'nai B'rith, it operated early on in New Mexico through the auspices of the regional office in Denver. Only in 1990, however, did

Albuquerque receive authorization for its own office, although it had operated at a high level of sensitivity even throughout the early decades after the war.

The level of anti-Semitism in New Mexico, despite the cited better known incidents, remained low. In 1988 the ADL report placed New Mexico, along with Montana, as having the lowest number of vandalistic events.[9] Although the early nineties showed some increase, by the mid-nineties those numbers had again fallen. Indeed, they were rare enough to suggest that the yearly increases and decreases could not readily be seen as a trend.

The ADL and other institutions kept a sharp eye on the positions of New Mexico's representatives in Congress. Its activism led its leaders into personal contact with the state's senators and members of the House of Representatives, where their votes on issues concerning Israel were monitored and commented upon. Some of their responses to Jewish New Mexicans found their way into the *Link*. Senator Pete Domenici replied to a letter from Jonathan Sutin in which he commented, "I hope you know, Jonathan, that now as always you may count on me to do all I can in support of Israel."[10] The contacts never ceased, even if the New Mexico delegation did not always affirm its position quite so readily.

The postwar issues produced a sharpness of focus among Jews nationally.[11] The creation of Israel and the perceived need for its security warranted a general support for the new state "as an embattled bastion of democracy."[12] For Jews generally, the necessity to find a place where their European brethren could reside and survive placed the survival of Israel at the top of issues that concerned them. Support for Israel also demanded that Jews speak out openly as Jews on the new country's behalf—an attitude that did not exist strongly before the war in New Mexico, although Zionism had had its firm advocates and opponents in both the northeast and New Mexico.

On the domestic front, in turn, defense of Jews concerning their own civil rights became part of a new national campaign to ensure rights for other beleaguered groups as well as for themselves in the name of fairness for all in America.[13] As never before, Jews organized and spoke up publicly on behalf of their own and others' causes. Such behavior was expressed more strongly in New Mexico than ever before. As early as 1958 Rabbi Shor of Congregation Albert sermonized the belief that Jews and Christians could survive only in righteous soil—with justice for all.[14] The minutes of the Albuquerque Jewish Welfare Fund show engagement in discussions that suggested that the organization should be more aggressive in supporting such issues as fair housing for blacks.[15] In the late forties and early fifties Jewish scientists at Los Alamos involved themselves in the name of the Anti-Defamation League on behalf of blacks and sought redress of grievances on matters of housing and even the right of blacks to receive haircuts on the base.[16] The battles that developed for the rights of blacks and women were embraced by many New Mexican Jews as an integral extension of their desire to gain fair play for themselves.

Such matters as abortion and a woman's right to choose gained much support from Jews generally and New Mexico's Jews reflected that position. Abortion became a burning national issue following the Supreme Court's *Roe v. Wade* decision upholding the procedure in 1973. Nationally, some thirty Protestant, Jewish, and other religious organizations formed the Religious Coalition for Abortion Rights (RCAR) in that year, supporting a pro-choice position.[17] In 1977 the Jewish Community Council of Albuquerque resolved to go on record as favoring freedom of choice with respect to abortion.[18] A year later it endorsed and became a sponsoring organization of the local chapter of the RCAR.[19] In 1989 the national American Jewish Committee (AJC) issued a statement in which it insisted that Jewish law found abortion to be "not murder and . . . mandatory where necessary to protect the life of the mother." It was, however, to be treated as "a course of last resort." The AJC pronounced its policy as "pro-choice, pro-family, pro-natalist."[20]

Not all branches of Judaism, however, held the same position in the matter. The Orthodox rabbinate held abortion permissible only in life-threatening situations for the mother, while the Reform branch upheld the need for legal and safe abortion based on personal choice. Differences with some Christian churches and between the Christian churches themselves, however, were much sharper.

Even in New Mexico, however, the pro-choice policy drew some unhappy reactions locally from groups that were presumably Christian. In 1989 Yom Kippur services found protesters in front of Temple Albert bearing signs with swastikas equating abortion and the Holocaust. Indeed, Rabbi Paul Citrin of Congregation Albert had been an active supporter of the right of a woman to choose. However, it was the first time such an action had been taken in front of a religious institution where abortion was not under discussion at the time and on the eve of one of the holiest days of the Jewish calendar. The protesters did not identify themselves as belonging to any leading anti-abortion organization. The rabbi found the incident minor even if "offensive and unrespectful."[21]

The event may be more important for the reaction it aroused in the broader population. Fifty local clergy representing mainstream Protestant churches and beyond (but not Baptists) expressed outrage at the demonstrators and some even defined the demonstration as anti-Semitic. Father Ernest Falardeau, a spokesman for the Catholic Archdiocese of Santa Fe, which strongly rejected abortion, but himself an active advocate of interfaith discussion, denied any connection of the protesters with church-sponsored organizations and reasserted the church's official and friendly relations with Congregation Albert.[22]

Other long-standing issues among Americans also came to the fore. The place of religion in the public schools had a considerable and varied history in New Mexico. The overwhelming historical presence of Catholic educational institutions had led to conflict as the territory and state sought to develop a public school system where only Catholic schools had existed previously. In the late forties and early fifties civil suits challenged and won decisions that disqualified Catholic clergy from teaching in public schools.[23] As part of the same rulings in 1949, eleven counties in New Mexico were found by the courts to be in violation of the separation of religion and state in matters involving free state-owned textbooks given to parochial schools and free transportation of church school children on public school buses. The court banned such practices. The skimpy reporting of these events in the *American Jewish Year Book* in the early decades after the war indicates that while New Mexico's Jews were interested in the subject, spirited participation by the Jewish community was not yet readily evident in those early decades.[24] Court decisions, however, did not end the matter either in practice or in legislative activity. Nevertheless, a new era of increased concern and openness came into being in which religion in the schools came into open question.

One would be less than generous, however, if one did not point out that the slow pace at which New Mexico faced the problem of creating a public education system at times left Jewish children in small communities in a position where the only education available to them outside of the home was in an existing Catholic school. The children of the Seligman family of Bernalillo, cousins Milton and Randolph, for example, both attended Catholic schools in their early years before the war and would, no doubt, have been forced to move to Albuquerque but for the church school presence.[25]

In time, such matters as the place of religion in public schools drew the ever more active attention of Jewish constituencies. Rabbi Shor, in an undated sermon, probably from the sixties, wondered about the reality of separation of church and state when six-year-old Jewish children came home singing "Little Lord Jesus."[26] Thus Jews sometimes found themselves siding with some Christian groups and opposed to others. The same circumstances occurred among Christian groups.

In later decades of the century the issue of religion continued to erupt in the public schools. In 1977 the Albuquerque Public School Board, after long consideration by a subcommittee that included the rabbis of the largest Jewish congregations, issued guidelines that it considered to be in accord with Supreme Court decisions involving religious issues. The principle of separation of church and state lay at the base of the policy and expressed itself in a policy of neutrality toward religion in public schools. The study of religion was deemed permissible only for "historical, artistic, cultural, literary," or secular purposes.[27] The issue, however, was a continuing one, despite the general satisfaction of the Jewish community with the outcome.

No small part of such differences continued to occur between Jews allied with mainstream Protestant religious groups against other Christians identified as the Christian "far right." The separation of church and state became one battleground with respect to school prayer. The Union of American Hebrew Congregations (UAHC) encouraged political action against organized prayer in the public schools in the mid-eighties. Rabbi Paul Citrin of Congregation Albert applauded the defeat in the New Mexico House Judiciary Committee of a resolution calling on Congress to amend the Constitution to allow prayer in the public schools, and he testified before the New Mexico House Judiciary Committee to that effect.[28] Several years later the rabbi spoke of his participation in a Committee of Religious Pluralism under the auspices of the New Mexico Council of Churches to maintain separation of church and state.[29] Rabbi Lynn Gottlieb drew the line at seeking guidelines that approved the study of religion but no sponsorship of religion by schools.[30] These matters received particular currency around the Christmas season. Jewish children felt the pressure of the heavily predominant Christian culture with particular force at that time.

The issue continued to have importance for the Jewish community throughout the late 1980s. In 1988 the Community Relations Council (CRC) of the JFGA hosted a conference on church-state issues that was cosponsored by, among others, the UNM Law

School, United Campus Ministries, and the Aquinas Newman Center. Jane Wishner, the chair of the CRC, placed such matters at the forefront of the local agenda.[31]

By late 1989 the Community Relations Council had formulated an "ideal" approach to the matter of the pervasiveness of Christmas celebration in the public schools. Seeking an approach that de-emphasized emphasis on religious holidays (including Chanukah), the CRC's statement sought to ensure the absence of religious symbols such as a tree or music recitals in order to avoid dividing or isolating children. Talking about religion as part of the educational process, however, was acceptable.[32]

Late in 1989 the Albuquerque public schools adopted guidelines on religious issues that appeared to ease concern. Working as a task force that included many groups, the JFGA and the Catholic archdiocese among them, they reached a consensus on the use of religious symbols such as the Christmas tree and on the view that the classroom should be neutral in religious matters. Although any precise measurement of how important Jewish participation may have been in reaching these conclusions is difficult, it is clear that Jewish institutions played an open and significant role in the deliberations, unlike their greater silence in the first decades after the war.

The actions of Albuquerque's city government and the Jewish community, however, did not prevent the state legislature from pursuing a different tack. In 1994 the latter passed memorials, without the force of law, which stressed the historical role of Jesus, who was described as embodying the Jewish prophetic and religious tradition, and sought a designation of November 21–27 as Christian Heritage Week. The ADL remained concerned with the action, seeing in it a possible avenue for increased religious activity in the public schools.[33] Jewish legislators remained aware of elements of religious activity in the House in the late 1990s. Although representatives denied the existence of open anti-Semitism, they admitted that the powerful environmental presence of Christianity permeated prayers. Jewish members of the legislature Denise Picraux and Rita Getty, both of Albuquerque districts, exercised caution in challenging the ritual at that time.[34]

Clearly, the religion/state issue was an ongoing one. However, it is difficult to imagine that the Jewish community would have ever engaged openly in such controversies on any level before World War II or even in the early decades after the war. The spirit injected into the community by the desire to stand up for itself expressed a bravery that grew out of a consciousness that it could not remain silent.

Nor did the religion/state issue end with holiday season practices. The matter of creation versus evolution also received public attention. On this issue differences appeared within the Jewish community itself as well as with certain Christian groups. Rabbi Shor, in an undated sermon, possibly from the sixties, stated his view succinctly: "Religion can no more deny the facts of science; science can neither prove nor disprove basic beliefs of religion." Even then the rabbi saw the major conflict as one between science and Bible fundamentalists.[35]

The views reflected conflicts occurring everywhere in the country. Rabbi Schmuckler of Chabad saw evolution as an antireligious stance that denied the existence of God. Conservative B'nai Israel's Rabbi Isaac Celnik, by contrast, viewed creation as a religious perspective and evolution as a scientific one. Reform Rabbi

Joseph Black of Congregation Albert saw in the anti-evolution stance an attempt to break down state-church divisions in favor of legislating belief and was in many respects in agreement with Rabbi Lynn Gottlieb, who viewed creationism as a religious interpretation of the Bible.[36] The issue arose over the state school board's setting of the core science curriculum without specifying evolution in the requirement. In 1997, State Senator Pauline Eisenstadt sponsored a bill specifying that evolution be taught in the sciences. The bill passed in the Senate but failed to do so in the House.[37]

New Mexico had its own unique set of historical features that old and new Jewish populations encountered on a common basis after World War II. The remnants of a Jewish past among some Hispanos began to emerge openly in New Mexico in the mid-1970s.[38] Their existence was the product of the forced religious conversion policy that dated back to the dictates of the Spanish Inquisition of the late fifteenth century. That action had led Spanish and Portuguese Jews to disperse in every direction. Eventually, with the spread of the Iberian population into the New World, hidden Jews or their descendants came to New Mexico.

Their presence was not completely unknown to the Anglo population after the American takeover of what became the American Southwest. There is some anecdotal evidence of marriage between Hispanic crypto- (secret) Jewish women and early German-Jewish settlers dating back to the nineteenth century. One must recall that early Jewish settlement had been almost exclusively by men, some of whom married Hispanic women because of the absence of Jewish females. The presence of crypto-Jews among the Hispanic population had been noted in popular literature at least as early as the mid-1950s.[39] Even earlier, Mary Austin, an author who settled in Santa Fe, noted in vague terms the presence of the descendants of Spanish Jews as early as 1919.[40]

The open disclosure of their existence by these hidden Jews, however, marked something new. It quickly fascinated New Mexico's Ashkenazic Jews as well as a broadening audience throughout the United States. In 1990 their existence reached the pages of the *New York Times*. The issues surrounding the validity and meaning of crypto-Jewish claims increasingly drew the attention of the scholarly community, while a growing literature on the subject appeared in the early eighties. The spectrum of opinion among scholars of a hidden Jewish presence was wide, extending from acceptance of the phenomenon as reality to outright denial. A prominent Catholic scholar of New Mexico genealogical history, Fray Angélico Chávez, wrote categorically in 1988 that "no Jews came to New Mexico in 1598–1600 and all during the Spanish period down to 1846. . . . Nor were there any Crypto-Jews."[41] Dr. Stanley M. Hordes, a historian and Jew living in New Mexico, stood at the other end of the spectrum of viewpoints and he published much to verify his stand.[42] The trend, however, judging by the weight of scholarship in the last years of the twentieth century, moved toward the ever greater acceptance of the reality of the presence of crypto-Judaism in New Mexico and of ever greater numbers of Hispanics openly claiming such heritage as their own.

Whether one accepts or denies the legitimacy of the claims of the crypto-Jews, a historian concentrating on the recent history of the Jews in New Mexico must still ask why this phenomenon, held secretly for centuries, came to light so quickly in the later twentieth century. A variety of circumstances might have contributed to this new condition. Hordes summarizes the reasons for its appearance in broad terms. The arrival of American rule brought a new political culture, new religious perspectives, and a new economy from the mid-1840s, which increasingly impacted the largely static Hispanic society. The relatively isolated rural population withstood some of that cultural onslaught longer than the growing urban areas. Additionally, the coming of public schools, television, and radio, as well as participation in World Wars I and II, jolted the traditional Hispanic culture from its old parameters.[43]

New Mexico's crypto-Jews well may have lost much of their knowledge of a Jewish heritage over the centuries since the Inquisition even if some customs (i.e., lighting candles on Friday evening, not eating pork) continued to be passed down within families, oftentimes for some without knowledge of why the practices existed. The Holocaust, too, may have incurred fears and denials. In the last decades of the twentieth century, however, they began to reveal themselves in their search for their own identity.

Neither can one ignore the question of the impact of a growing presence of Ashkenazic transplants in the postwar period and its effects upon the hidden Jews. Hordes himself, when serving as state historian in the early 1980s, noted that persons confessing a crypto-Jewish heritage appeared in his office to reveal their claims.[44] Those Hispanos seeking to emerge from their secretive state also turned to rabbis and Jewish acquaintances as their first open steps in breaking with the silence of the past. If nothing else, the open presence of the Ashkenazim became a vehicle for transmitting their questions and hopes. The ever-increasing interaction of traditional Hispano and Anglo societies allowed the Jewish Hispanos to break more readily with their own isolation and secrecy.

Some of those Hispanos who openly declared themselves Jews joined existing congregations. Congregation Nahalat Shalom even held monthly services in Ladino, the folk language of Hispanic Jews.[45] Rabbi Issac Celnik, long-time rabbi at Congregation B'nai Israel, interviewed in 1990, spoke of cautious contacts initiated with him by Hispanic persons with belief in their Jewish background in the late 1900s after he had been in Albuquerque nearly twenty years. They either sat alone at services or invited him to come to their homes.[46] And Rabbi Paul Citrin of Congregation Albert spoke of his surprise at finding such persons in his congregation in the late 1970s when he took up his ministerial duties in Albuquerque. His training, he confessed, had not prepared him for their existence.[47]

Although New Mexico Hispanos in general adopted a variety of views toward the existence of Jewish elements in their midst, a segment of their society has accepted the presence of a Jewish past and even a Jewish present. Such Hispanic publications as *La Herencia del Norte* (*The Heritage of the North*) in the nineties devoted considerable space to articles about crypto-Judaism and Sephardic customs. The editors also published numerous responses to those articles in letters to the editor. They range from surprise at learning that their backgrounds might include Jewish elements to reevaluation of memories of family customs to claims of a "giant tidal wave of revelation that is being exposed to Hispanics of Sephardic descent," leading to the "springing up" of Sephardic Messianic congregations.[48]

Some New Mexico Hispanics moved beyond reliance on Anglo Jews to discover themselves. Dennis Duran, a Hispano who formally converted to Judaism in 1977, created an organization in 1994 called

Anusim Yisrael (The Forced Ones of Israel) to aid those who sought to find out about a Jewish or suspected Jewish past and how to come to terms with it. In late 1997 meetings were limited to Sephardic Jews out of a tendency among them to remain silent when outsiders were present. At that time, it had some fifty members.[49]

It goes beyond the realm of the historian to foresee the future course of such developments. However, at the turn of the new century the interest in and opening up of some Hispanos to their own past certainly led to contacts and realization of ties between the Ashkenazic Jews of New Mexico and those of a hidden Sephardic past. Nevertheless, great cultural gaps remain. The social experience of crypto-Judaism in its hidden and Hispanic form still often separated its practitioners from an open practice and social life with the recent American Jewish immigrants to New Mexico. It is clear, however, that the Ashkenazic Jewish community that lived in the state in 1940 had, at best, little or no knowledge of crypto-Judaism and either found it strange or simply refused to talk about it. By the year 2000 the subject had attracted considerable attention among New Mexico's Jews and Jewish and Christian scholars both in and far beyond the state's boundaries.

The intensity of New Mexico Jews' awareness of themselves and their relation to the non-Jewish environment in which they lived can be seen in the internal debate that took place over placing a monument to the Holocaust in Albuquerque's Civic Plaza. In 1980 a memorial plaque and six trees had been planted in memory of the six million victims of the Holocaust. Mayor David Rusk read the memorial. When the city decided to renovate the plaza in 1995 the location of the memorial had to be changed.

In accord with the new circumstances, city authorities approached the Federation with respect to the fate of the memorial. The notion of a new, much larger sculpture arose and the city authorities accepted it. Along with it, however, came sharp differences of opinion within the Jewish community itself. Some

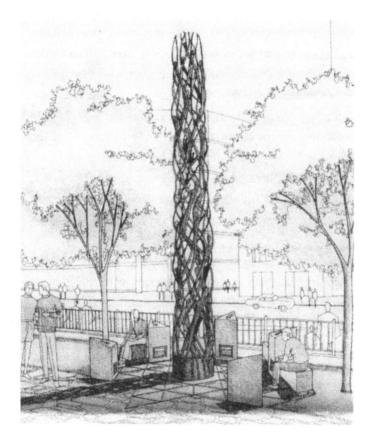

FIGURE 18. Drawing of Holocaust memorial by sculptor Jake Lovato of bodies rising in a smoke stack. Courtesy of the *Link*.

questioned the appropriateness of the location. The plaza was a place of celebration. Others pondered the issue of location in relation to that of religion and state. Among the critics were concentration camp survivors who feared an anti-Semitic backlash.[50] The Federation, however, insisted on keeping the location.

The design itself aroused another dimension of discussion. Arrived at through open competition, Jake Lovato, the sculptor, created a column, originally twenty feet high, of human silhouettes spiraling upward as a smokestack. Some survivors of the camps found it too painful, although the design was retained. Mayor Martin Chavez objected to the twenty-foot height of the memorial, fearing it would dominate the landscape. The city and the Federation compromised at fifteen and one-half feet.[51] The dichotomy of fear by some and insistence on being open and direct by others was indicative of the ever-present insecurity, particularly by those who had suffered cruelly, and the assertiveness of the younger, organized elements of the Jewish population.

Over the course of the half century since World War II the issues that confronted Jews in New Mexico were mostly national in nature. Generally, Jews in New Mexico did not face them alone and, over the decades, expressed themselves openly and actively as never before. Given the increasing contact between themselves and other religious communities, the prospects for solving problems grew greater than they had been before World War II.

CHAPTER EIGHT

The Jewish Presence

*T*he modest self-identification that characterized the behavior of the prewar Jews operated to obscure their presence. It was after World War II, as noted, that Jewish newcomers became aware of a Jewish past in New Mexico and served as the principal agents to bring it to light. The perceived new demands they made upon themselves in New Mexico, fostered by their new problems, the Holocaust, and the creation of Israel, as well as by their increasing numbers and the breaking of the state's isolation, allowed a new kind of presence to emerge. Not only did they play new roles in society, but the atmosphere of openness and tolerance welcomed them to engage as never before in a greater range of activity, breaking from the narrower parameters of the past.

No small element in the new openness was the result of the discovery by the new Jewish immigrants of a Jewish past in New Mexico. Old-timers were, perhaps, too modest or cautious to single themselves out in terms of their historical importance. Older Anglo historians, too, may have overlooked the existence of subgroups within their midst as a result of their own definitions of identity. Thus prewar Anglo historians of New Mexico may have presented Anglos as a unified group while postwar changes of attitude, fed by increased numbers, led the subgroups to look more closely at their own identity and history.

The great population growth in the state through immigration brought in varied peoples whose presence slowly moved New Mexico beyond the simplified old triple image of Anglo, Hispano, and American Indian. Anglos, in particular, reflected the varieties that existed among themselves elsewhere—where the term "Anglo" was unknown as used in New Mexico. The entire range of religious expression, economic production, and available culture broadened, allowing nuances to be seen that had been unseen or unused before the war.

For Jews, the contents of *New Mexico Magazine*, a journal that touted the beautiful scenery and the unique cultural characteristics of the old indigenous population, portrays one example of the change. Before World War II it published no articles on a Jewish presence. Between 1975 and 2000, however, a number of articles appeared in which Jews or Judaism were specifically featured. The subject matter ranged from description of religious holidays to depiction of pioneer families, to the appearance of Jews in cultural areas new to them in New Mexico, to the presence of crypto-Jews. Considering their still small numbers in the total population, the attention they warranted from the magazine was noteworthy. Only the Lebanese and Italians warranted single articles of their own in the journal. My intent here is to point out the greatly increased interest of the Jews themselves in their New Mexican past and their willingness to share it openly. Many of the authors of the articles were of the Jewish faith. The magazine also reflected the increased interest of the non-Jewish population in the Jews in their midst.

The new areas of participation for Jews expanded greatly. They began to take part in activities in which they had had no previous presence, or virtually none. Considerations of space allow only a few examples of their presence to be noted. Yet, given their small numbers, the breadth of their expanded activities is impressive.

The arts present one such dimension of this increased visibility. Unlike their significant role in the economic development of Anglo New Mexico before World War II, Jews had taken a decidedly lesser role in cultural matters. Yet their participation was not without importance in an economic sense. As early as 1882 Jake Gold, in Santa Fe, had a shop featuring Native American pottery—then called curios—and Abe Spiegelberg's shop in the capital featured such items by the late nineteenth century. They preceded Anglo artists' groups that were just beginning to arrive on the Taos scene at the end of the nineteenth century. Abe Spiegelberg had even written an article about Navajo blankets in 1904.[1] He was enough of a fixture that artist B. J. O. Nordfeldt produced a well-known portrait of him in 1919, which hangs in the lobby of the La Fonda hotel in Santa Fe.[2] Herman Schweitzer, based in Albuquerque as superintendent of Fred Harvey's News and Curio Department from 1901 to 1943, was dubbed the "patriarch of the modern Indian crafts business."[3] In 1915 Julius Gans organized the Southwest Arts and Crafts Company in Santa Fe, which both manufactured and sold Native American rugs and jewelry. If not artists themselves, Jews had clearly been present in the commerce of the emerging world of Native arts.

But the artistic scene was changing. In the world of art producers, rather than sellers, perhaps the first artist who was a Jew to appear on the New Mexico scene (briefly) was Maurice Sterne. The husband (also briefly) of Mabel Dodge Luhan, who would play a powerful role in attracting artists and writers to New Mexico in the period between the First and Second World Wars, he was a recognized artist of merit. The two divorced, however, and he left New Mexico.

Sterne's major importance for the arts in New Mexico may lie in his role of persuading his wife to come to the state. In 1917 he wrote to her, "Dearest Girl, Do you want an object in life? Save the Indians, their art culture—reveal it to the world."[4] Shortly afterward she appeared in Santa Fe and, unhappy with its cultural atmosphere, quickly moved to Taos, where she helped to create one of the state's major centers of cultural developments before World War II.

In the postwar era, practicing Jewish artists appeared on the New Mexico scene with increasing frequency.[5] Space allows only an illustrative smattering of names. One of the earliest of the postwar era was Ira Moskowitz, who lived in New Mexico from 1944 to 1955. Along with his wife, Anna Barry, they tasted the local artistic culture and then, typical of their peripatetic life-style, moved on.

Among the more permanent and unique was Arthur (Art) Sussman, who came to Albuquerque in the early sixties and stayed. Unlike many artists who were overwhelmed by local scenery and Native Americans in their work, he remained inspired by Old Testament subject matter and occasionally turned to American Indian images as inspiration for his work.

FIGURE 19. Artist Art Sussman. Courtesy of the *Link*.

Perhaps the best-known art producer was Judy Chicago, who came to New Mexico in the early eighties. She was an important national figure in the development of the feminist movement in art in the seventies. Her complex work *The Dinner Party*, which highlighted women omitted from history, became permanently displayed at the Brooklyn Museum in 2007. In 1993 another of her works, the *Holocaust Project*, premiered in Chicago after years of preparation and travel as an exhibit throughout the United States. In concert with her pursuit of the Holocaust, Judy Chicago pursued her personal discovery of her own Judaism with Rabbi Lynn Gottlieb.[6] After some years in Santa Fe, with which she became disenchanted, she settled with her husband in Belen, some thirty miles south of Albuquerque.

The post-eighties generation witnessed an increasing presence of artists dedicated to Jewish themes in their work. In Santa Fe, Sara Novenson combined biblical matriarchs and bright colors into her painting that moved well beyond the traditional southwestern

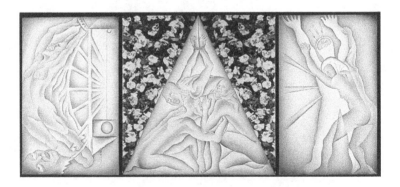

FIGURE 20. Pink Triangle/Torture, Judy Chicago, 1993.
Photo by Donald Woodman.

context.[7] She opened a gallery on Canyon Road in Santa Fe. In Albuquerque, the Bashert Gallery in Old Town, with equal insistence, dedicated itself to displaying Judaica in the belief that a market existed for it.[8]

Nor were they alone. Other Jewish artists boldly displayed their work in galleries around town, making it evident that they had arrived in New Mexico. By 1995 groups of Jewish artists were combining to display their works at the National Hispanic Cultural Center. Among the exhibits were ceramics that combined Jewish ceremonial objects influenced by pueblo pottery traditions. Another exhibiter, Cary Herz, showed her photographs of crypto-Jewish gravestones, a possible addition to the arguments supporting the case for the presence of hidden Jews.[9]

The presence of Jewish writers also became a reality in postwar New Mexico. Mark Medoff, the author of *Children of a Lesser God*, established himself on the faculty of New Mexico State University in Las Cruces. Albuquerque could claim the residence of Henry Roth, whose work *Call It Sleep* belatedly attracted national attention. In the seventies Roth emerged enough from his obscurity to become an active member of the editorial board of the *Link*. These writers formed a new dimension of the Jewish presence even though their best-known works did not center around the state and its culture.

In music, too, Jews moved onto the New Mexico scene. On the national scene they had long made a mark in popular and classical music—both as composers and as musicians. In 1985 the New Mexico Symphony Orchestra, then a new institution, appointed Neal Stulberg to the post of conductor. He came from Los Angeles, where he had been an assistant conductor of that city's orchestra.[10]

Still quite young, Stulberg stayed until 1992. He earned praise for his adventurous programming, despite the financially starved condition of the orchestra.[11] The peripatetic character of his occupation then took him to many posts in Europe and Israel. His stop in Albuquerque, however, marked a new and highly visible step in the broadening presence of Jews on the New Mexico cultural scene.

In their mass migrations to America, their distinctive or preferred foods accompanied the Jews into the New World, a process also adopted by many of the other new immigrants. While the prewar Jews in New Mexico, few in number, generally adopted the eating habits of their environment as part of their own, their desire for accustomed foods did not disappear and the need to follow the dictates of religious tradition demanded outside supply. The issue of kosher food was scarcely a matter of general communal concern, but there were those who had long imported such products for themselves. Even in the early postwar period, in advertising for a cantor–Hebrew teacher in the 1950s, a B'nai Israel form letter noted, "We do not have any Kosher meat facilities in the city as there are only twelve families who observe kasruth." They ordered supplies from Denver or Tucson.[12] At that time, the advertisement claimed, there were 180 members in the congregation. With the large-scale postwar immigration from the older Jewish centers of the Northeast, the matter gradually became more important, visible, and feasible from the economic viewpoint.

While strictly kosher foods were still the concern of only a small minority, foods reminiscent of the eastern United States became ever more sought after and obtainable. As early as 1943 Magidson's restaurant in downtown Albuquerque, then the center of the city, readily attracted eastern newcomers with its delicatessen-type foods. Steady customers had sandwiches named after themselves. A visiting professor from New York at the University of New Mexico described it as a place "where nostalgic Easterners convene for real pastrami."[13] Milton Seligman described it as "a great gathering place for Jews who were going to talk about fundraising or how much somebody didn't give to charity."[14] Kosher food was obtainable there and into the 1980s, by which time the restaurant had moved into the rapidly developing Northeast Heights. The early restaurant may have been the first "hangout" for Jews in the city.

Increasing numbers led to improved sources of supply. By the early sixties Dave's Kosher Meats (and borscht) arrived on the scene. The Kosher Co-op came into existence in the late sixties and in the late eighties had some 150 members.[15] Stores in the bread and bakery line also made an appearance. By the sixties the supermarket had entered the picture. The Nob Hill Super Market, purchased by Milton Greenberg in 1964, created an entire kosher department with 150 items. By 1983, under Paul Schultz, it carried nearly 300 products. In the late eighties, however, no restaurant in Albuquerque yet carried full authorization as kosher.[16]

In 1994, another step was taken when the creation of a supervised certified kosher dairy restaurant became a reality. Wolfe's Bagels received its legitimacy through Chabad Rabbi Chaim Schmukler. Although the owners did not claim their changed status on the basis of large-scale demand, they did find sufficient interest, as well as the power of their own inclinations, to undergo the difficult and costly process of kashrut.

Santa Fe, too, responded to the desire for kosher food. The growing presence of an Orthodox population proved a driving force. Santa Fe's tendency toward the use of health foods made the process relatively easy. Santa Fe's Jews also created a kosher cooperative, Midbar Co-op, which made it possible to obtain items not readily obtainable elsewhere.[17]

One of the traditional food icons associated with the Jews, the bagel, became increasingly popular in New Mexico in the postwar era. Apparently created originally in the seventeenth century to commemorate the victory of a Polish king over the Turks, it had spread throughout eastern Europe and migrated to the United States with the mass immigration between the 1880s and the 1920s. By 1920 cream cheese had been added as a spread. In the postwar era, freezing techniques led to nationwide marketing. Usage spread as meats were added for variety. Fittingly, in New Mexico, chile, a New Mexican staple, made its way into the product. By 1993 the *Link* noted the bagel's boom. Four bagel makers existed in Albuquerque alone.[18] Beyond bagels, the latke, a potato pancake popular among Jews, acquired the addition of salsa where previously sour cream or applesauce had sufficed. It was a New Mexican version of a "melting pot."

The participation of Jews in New Mexico's political life was a fact of long standing before World War II. Their ambitions in office holding were largely limited to county and city positions. Albuquerque's first mayors in the late 1880s and early 1890s were Jews. The highest rung of the political ladder a Jew reached before World War II had been the election of Arthur Seligman of Santa Fe, a Democrat, to the governorship in 1930. Seligman's Jewish lineage was quite clear but his own adherence to the Jewish community less so.

In the early postwar decades Jews continued to seek and hold local political office. Among the early postwar officeholders was

FIGURE 21. Steve Schiff. Courtesy of Steve Schiff Campaign 1996.

Milton Seligman, a native New Mexican, who was elected to the state legislature from Sandoval County. More impressive changes came in the 1980s. In 1988 Steve Schiff of Albuquerque, a newcomer who built up a long resume of government legal office holding, was elected to the U.S. House of Representatives on the Republican ticket. His popularity was impressive, growing from 51 percent of the vote in his first victory to 70 percent in 1990.[19] He was reelected in 1994 and was in his fifth term when he died, a victim of cancer, in 1998.

Schiff, a member of Congregation Albert, took positions that stood on the side of Israel. An advertisement in the *Link* of October 1990 announced that we (Jews) should "Reelect our Congressman" and described him as "our voice in Washington."[20] As a moderate Republican, he supported a woman's right to choose in the matter of abortion, and held that homosexuals should serve in combat duty.[21] The *Albuquerque Journal* supported him editorially. He was also a target of skinhead slurs on the basis of his Judaism.[22] Congressman Schiff proved to be a popular representative of all the people of his district and his openly Jewish background added a new place to the Jewish presence in New Mexico.

A new dimension of Jewish political presence also appeared with the election of Pauline Eisenstadt to the New Mexico House of Representatives. She served in the House between 1984 and 1992 and in the state senate from 1996 to 2000. Up to that point she was the only woman elected to both houses of the legislature. In the late nineties, three Jews were serving in the legislature.

The appointment of Joseph Polisar as police chief in Albuquerque also broke new ground in the 1990s. Raised in Great Neck, New York, he joined the Albuquerque police department in 1977. Polisar recalled that as a Jew his awareness of minority concerns served

FIGURE 22. State Representative and Senator Pauline Eisenstadt.
Courtesy of the *Link*.

him well. He fostered dialogue between minorities and the police and in 1996 earned the Martin Luther King Jr. "Keep the Dream Alive" award from the black community. A year earlier he had been honored by the Albuquerque Human Rights Board for improving police and minority relations.[23]

Despite his public visibility, knowledge of Polisar's religious background appears to have been scarce. Upon the death of Yitzhak Rabin he offered some remarks at the memorial for the deceased Israeli leader. Polisar noted that after that he received hate mail, presumably as public awareness of his background grew.[24] Nevertheless, a Jew respected by a metropolitan police department also presented a new dimension of the Jewish presence in New Mexico. Polisar's term came to an end in 1998 following the election of a new mayor in that year.

Although national elections went beyond the boundaries of New Mexico, the selection of Senator Joseph Lieberman as candidate for vice-president in 2000 also provided a new and high moment for New Mexico's Jews. One comment by Rabbi Lynn Gottlieb summed up the mood. "The Jewish community is starting to move out of the trauma . . . that made our hearts heavy after the Holocaust. We're in a period of confidence. . . . And this has been made most manifest by Senator Lieberman being named as candidate."[25] Rabbi Schmuckler saw Lieberman's selection as a sign that Jews did not need to conceal their Jewishness.[26] Even the Democratic Party's loss of the election did not erase the feeling of elation at his choice.

In the nineteenth century—before the coming of the railroad in 1880—Jews had created some of the most successful business enterprises in the New Mexico Territory. They often combined retail and wholesale operations and often linked American Indian reservations and the army with supplies obtained in New Mexico or from the East. Some were already making their mark before the Civil War and flourished greatly afterward. The names of Spiegelberg, Staab, and Ilfeld had ranked among the most successful of them.

The arrival of the railroad changed business practices sharply and led to the decline of many such widespread enterprises after 1880. Jewish newcomers continued to be entrepreneurs although the large majority of the businesses were much smaller than their predecessors of prerailroad days. The activities of the Ilfeld family, however, were an exception to this rule down to World War II. The closer one comes to 1940, the greater the degree of specialization appeared to be. This process continued into the postwar world. Some of the largest Jewish-owned businesses followed this path.

A few examples of this process in the immediate postwar years follow. The sharp demand for housing amid the rapid growth of Albuquerque in the first postwar decades saw the appearance of Sam Hoffman as a home builder. By 1954 he ranked as the third-largest home builder in the United States. Operating in other towns, Hoffman constructed multiple dwellings in Phoenix. Tragically, he committed suicide in 1959 on the eve of starting a new mass project on Albuquerque's West Side.[27] Hoffmantown, in Albuquerque, remains as a monument to his enterprise.

Albuquerque's growth also received a Jewish name of distinction in the person of architect Max Flatow. Arriving in 1947 via his work on the Manhattan Project, Flatow established himself by designing government buildings, some of the tallest structures in

the growing city, and a modern style suited to its rapid expansion—
"away from the kind of Disneyland romanticism of Santa Fe," as
a dean of the University of New Mexico's School of Architecture
described it.[28] His body of work included the First National Bank
building, the College of Education complex at the university, the
Marriott Hotel, and numerous government structures. He retired
in 1990.

Another success story began with the furniture retail business
of Emanual Blaugrund. Under the name of American Furniture, he
initiated his enterprise in 1936. An immigrant raised in Czechoslo-
vakia, he joined his brothers in El Paso and subsequently moved to
Albuquerque. Originally located in the city's downtown, where his
store held some 40,000 square feet in 1968, the enterprise moved
to the rapidly expanding east side of town where the main store
occupied some 160,000 square feet. The business kept pace with
the expansion of the city's home building and population growth.
It remained the largest outlet of its kind within the city and by the
mid-nineties had expanded to Santa Fe, Farmington, and Tucson.
His sons, Lee and Cliff, subsequently took over the business.

The building boom of the first postwar decades also abetted
the creation of the Duke City Lumber Company. It was founded
by Maurice Liberman and Joe and Jack Grevey in 1945 and became
the largest lumber business in New Mexico. The founders were
all newcomers to Albuquerque. In 1968 they sold the business to
U.S. Industries.[29]

Not all the estimable work of New Mexico's Jews stemmed
from newcomers. The heritage of the Ilfeld Company, which dated
from the immediate post–Civil War era, extended well into the
twentieth century. Charles Ilfeld's partner and brother-in-law, Max

Nordhaus, had moved the headquarters of business operations to Albuquerque in 1911. Robert Nordhaus, son of Max and Bertha Staab Nordhaus, became a distinguished attorney in the city. In the post–World War II era he, with Ben Abruzzo, was a major figure in the creation of the Sandia Park Aerial Tramway and the Sandia Ski Area on the east side of the mountain. Robert became deeply involved in Native American affairs as an attorney for the Jicarilla Apaches and he was made an honorary member of the tribe for his thirty years of effort on the their behalf.[30]

And quietly, there were persons who contributed heavily to the health and welfare of New Mexican society. Dr. Randolph Seligman, a native son born in Bernalillo and perhaps the first Jewish ob-gyn in New Mexico, saw to the birth of close to 10,000 children in his career, beginning in 1949 and ending in 1996. The medical school established a professorship in his name.

Knowledge about Jews—both for Jews and for the general public—made considerable strides in the postwar world. As ethnic and racial issues came to the fore, Jews set forth claims to their own niche in the field of formal education. In the early seventies black and Hispanic studies programs appeared at the University of New Mexico and Jewish students, perhaps following their example, sought to strengthen their own identity. Courses on Jewish subject matter appeared in the curriculum at the behest of Jewish students and the availability of Jewish professors to offer them. Professor Gunther Rothenberg of the History Department initiated such courses and in time Professor Noel Pugach continued and expanded them. By the end of the century courses ranged from the general history of the Jews and the Jews in America to the availability of Hebrew language study and examinations of Old Testament history. Student enrollment continued to justify their existence. Nevertheless, university courses, however important, could reach only a limited number of people. The organized community also sought to reach out to a wider audience through educational programs, lectures, and discussions.[31]

The limitations on space have allowed only a cursory glance at the scope of Jewish participation in the state's development. It is clear, however, that this participation expanded broadly on the cultural and professional scene while maintaining a creditable continuation of its merchant past. The picture was an optimistic one.

Conclusions and Afterthoughts

$\mathcal{F}$or Jewish residents living in New Mexico before World War II, as for all other New Mexicans, the changes brought about by the war must have been astonishing. How could they have conceived of a Los Alamos and what it brought in its wake! One could say the same for the Sandia Corporation or Kirtland Field in Albuquerque and other bases scattered throughout the state. The enormous growth of an Albuquerque and a Rio Rancho leaves old-timers shaking their heads.

If one compares the period covered in this work with that of the prewar history of the Jews in New Mexico, the differences appear startling and clear. The changes allow the conclusion that as New Mexico changed so did the Jewish community. Both the state and its Jewish population showed a rapid increase in population. However, as a still relatively small group, the changes that occurred among the Jews were even greater than those experienced by the state as a whole. Not only did the number of religious institutions they created increase prodigiously, but the narrow range of religious practice that had existed before the war broadened to include a great part of the spectrum practiced by American Jews nationally. Additionally, a virtually new dimension of secular organizations to serve the community became a fact of Jewish life in New Mexico.

And then there was the change of mood among the Jews. They became a community that expressed itself publicly from one that had maintained a relatively discreet silence. It was the new conditions that faced them in the postwar period that placed upon them the need to stand for themselves. That became evident in the number and variety of institutions that appeared in the postwar world for Jews everywhere and were replicated in even greater degree in New Mexico. The new population that arrived joined with the relatively small older population to display an activism in support of the new causes that had arisen out of the war and on behalf of broader national issues, such as civil rights, that had been relatively muted or had received relatively little organized attention prior to the war.

The increase in Jewish numbers that accompanied the economic changes in New Mexico permitted an expansion in the social composition of the community. The merchant society of prewar days became one that included professionals of all kinds. The changes also involved a wider range of behavior toward the general population. Before the war, for example, the Jewish merchants often remained tied to a customer base that required that they adapt themselves to the cultural presence of the majority of their customers. The new economy created a choice of occupation not present before the war and an independence that allowed voices to be heard where silence had often been the rule.

The blossoming of Jewish society in the half century since World War II must appear historically as a time of good fortune for them. One must bear in mind, however, that the year 2000, for all the noteworthiness of the completion of the Jewish Community Center, does not mark either the end of an old or the beginning of a new era despite the changes that have taken place. Following the dramatic changes brought about by the war itself in New Mexico and upon the composition of Jewish society as a result of it, an evolutionary process took place, which, while powerful, could not match equally the distinct causes such as had been created by the war. However, such changes as brought about by feminism, strengthened activism, secular and religious institutional growth, interfaith relations, and an aging population expressed themselves in an evolutionary form that has become increasingly important since the war but lacks the drama brought about by the war. It has been a remarkable half century.

Appendix

Congregations Listed in the *Link*, August 2000

Albuquerque Area

    Chabad of New Mexico, Traditional

    Chavurat Hamidbar, Independent Traditional

    Congregation Albert, Reform

    Congregation B'nai Israel, Conservative

    Nahalat Shalom, Jewish Renewal/Independent

    New Mexico Community for Humanistic Judaism, Humanistic

    Rio Rancho Jewish Center, Conservative

Congregations Around the State

    Chabad Jewish Center of Santa Fe

    Chavurah Kol HaLev, Renewal, Santa Fe

    Congregation Beit Tikva, Traditional Reform, Santa Fe

    Pardes Yisroel, Orthodox, Santa Fe

    Temple Beth Shalom, Reform

    Jewish Community of Las Vegas

    B'nai Israel of Roswell

Carlsbad Jewish Congregation

Congregation Mishkan Shalom, Reconstructionist Congregation
for Southeastern New Mexico

Havurah B'nai Shalom, Ranchos de Taos

Los Alamos Jewish Center

Walking Stick Retreat Center, Cuba

Temple Beth El, Reform, Las Cruces

Notes

Chapter 2

1. U.S. Department of Commerce, *Population, 1940* (Washington, DC: Bureau of the Census, 1941), 1; U.S. Department of Commerce, "New Mexico," *1970 Census of Population* (Washington, DC: Bureau of the Census), table 17, 33–32.

2. Mid-Region Council of Governments of New Mexico, *Summary of 2000 Census Sample Data*, part 2: *Census Tract Data*, Albuquerque, New Mexico, December 2002, 2.

3. The *American Jewish Year Book* is a directory of information concerning Jews with respect to events and statistics of the year published. It also contains scholarly articles. For most of its existence the *Year Book* was published in Philadelphia, then jointly for a time in Philadelphia and New York. Since 1994, New York has been the sole place of publication by the American Jewish Committee. The *Year Book* citation henceforth will be *AJYB*.

4. *AJYB* 100 (2000): 246.

5. *AJYB* 42 (1940–41): 222; *AJYB* 100 (2000): 247.

6. *AJYB* 42 (1940–41): 228; *AJYB* 62 (1961): 62; *AJYB* 82 (1982): 67–68; *AJYB* 100 (2000): 255.

7. U.S. Department of Commerce, *Census of Population: 1960*, vol. 1 (Washington, DC: Bureau of the Census, 1961), 33–37.

8. Bureau of Business and Economic Research (BBER), "City Population from the U.S. Bureau of the Census: New Mexico City Population." Compiled from U.S. Department of Commerce, Bureau of the Census (Albuquerque: BBER, University of New Mexico, June 7, 2002).

9. *AJYB* 42 (1940–41): 253; *AJYB* 74 (1973): 312.

10. *AJYB* 100 (2000): 255.

11. BBER, "City Population."

12. See Henry J. Tobias and Charles E. Woodhouse, *Santa Fe: A Modern History, 1880–1990* (Albuquerque: University of New Mexico Press, 2001), 126.

13. Leah Kellogg, "Santa Fe, 1950 to 1975" (talk given to New Mexico Jewish Historical Society, 2002), 2.

14. *AJYB* 42 (1940–41): 253.

15. *AJYB* 74 (1973): 312; "The Santa Fe Jewish Community in 1967," ms. in author's possession.

16. "The Santa Fe Jewish Community in 1967."

17. Temple Beth Shalom, *Membership List*, October 1981.

18. Temple Beth Shalom, *Membership Directory and Yellow Pages*, 2001.

19. *AJYB* 100 (2000): 255.

20. U.S. Department of Commerce, *Census of Population: 1950*, vol. 1 (Washington, DC: Bureau of the Census, 1952), 31–36; U.S. Department of Commerce, *1980 Census of Population*, vol. 1 (Washington, DC: Bureau of the Census, January 1982), 33-13; BBER, "City Population."

21. *AJYB* 100 (2000): 255.

22. U.S. Department of Commerce, *Census of Population: 1950*, 31–36.

23. U.S. Department of Commerce, *1980 Census of Population*, vol. 1, part 33, "New Mexico," 33–38; BBER, "City Population."

24. The *New Mexico Jewish Link* 26, no. 11 (December 1997): 1. Henceforth cited as the *Link*. Quoting Jay Wechsler, Manhattan Project physicist.

25. Paul Sperling, "Jews of Early Los Alamos," *Western States Jewish Quarterly* 18, no. 4 (July 1986): 355.

26. Abraham I. Shinedling, "History of the Los Alamos Jewish Center, Los Alamos, New Mexico (1944 to 1957)," Albuquerque, 1958, 4–6, in author's possession.

27. *AJYB* 91 (1991): 215.

28. *AJYB* 100 (2000): 255.

29. David H. Morrissey, "The Little Tract That Grew," *Albuquerque Journal Magazine*, December 30, 1986, 4. See also chapter 5, "Congregational Growth and Religious Change."

30. Rio Rancho Jewish Center scrapbooks, Rio Rancho, New Mexico.

31. *Link* 27, no. 2 (February 1998): 12.

32. *Link* 31, no. 8 (September 2002): 4, 6.

33. *Link* 17, no. 3 (March 1988): 3.

34. *Link* 31, no. 8 (September 2002): 1, 14.

35. Iris Keltz, "Searching for a Village: A Wandering Jew in the Counter Culture" (paper given at the New Mexico Jewish Historical Society, 15th Annual Conference, November 8–10, 2002).

36. *Link* 31, no. 5 (May 2002): 1, 7.

37. *AJYB* 42 (1940–41): 253.

Chapter 3

1. Ted Bartimus and Scott McCartney, *Trinity's Children* (New York: Harcourt, 1991), 111.

2. Necah Stewart Furman, *Sandia National Laboratories: The Postwar Decade* (Albuquerque: University of New Mexico Press, 1990), 453.

3. Gerald D. Nash, *The American West in the Twentieth Century* (Englewood Cliffs, NJ: Prentice-Hall, 1973), 219.

4. *The UNM Catalog* (Albuquerque: University of New Mexico, 1999–2001), 12–13, 429, 433; Michael Welsh, "A Land of Extremes: The Economy of Modern New Mexico, 1940–1990," in *Contemporary New Mexico, 1940–1990*, ed. Richard Etulain (Albuquerque: University of New Mexico Press, 1994), 81.

5. Jewish Community Council, "1978 Campaign," untitled papers.

6. Gunther E. Rothenberg, "JSU," *Out of the Desert* 2, no. 1 (Winter 1971–72): 7.

7. *Link* 29, no. 11 (December 1998): 1, 12–13.

8. Howard M. Sachar, *A History of the Jews in the Modern World* (New York: Random House, 2005), 693.

9. For a fuller description see Henry J. Tobias, *A History of the Jews in New Mexico* (Albuquerque: University of New Mexico Press, 1990), 174–77.

10. Congregation B'nai Israel, August 8, 1941.

11. Ibid.; "Confidential Information: Congregation B'nai Israel Membership List, October 1965."

12. Israel C. Carmel Archive, Congregation Albert, 1950–51.

13. This table is used in Tobias, *History*, 176, with data for the year 2000 added in column 4. The new column is based on Congregation Albert membership. B'nai Israel data were unavailable except in quite fragmentary form. Even that small amount of data indicated a content roughly similar to Congregation Albert's. The figures do not include retirees.

14. Congregation Albert, *Membership Directory, 2000–2001*.

15. Brian McDonald, David Boldt, and Lawrence A. Waldman, *The New Mexico Economy: History and Outlook* (Albuquerque: BBER, January 1994), 28.

16. Congregation B'nai Israel *Year Book*, 1980–81; Congregation B'nai Israel, *Year Book*, 5762 (2001).

17. Santa Fe Jewish Temple and Community Center, Inc., "Membership List," 1968.

18. Ibid.; Temple Beth Shalom, *Membership List*, October 1981.

19. See Tobias, *History*, 177–78.

20. Congregation Albert and Auxiliaries, *Year Book*, 1980–1981; Congregation Albert, *Membership Directory*, 2000–2001.

21. Temple Beth Shalom, *Membership List*, October 1981; Temple Beth Shalom, *Membership Directory and Yellow Pages*, 2001.

22. Temple Beth Shalom, *Membership Directory and Yellow Pages*, 2001.

23. Congregation Albert and Auxiliaries, *Year Book*, 1980–81; Congregation Albert, *Membership Directory*, 2000–2001.

24. The author used telephone books and congregation membership lists to make compilations.

25. *Link* 2, no. 7 (March 1973): 3.

26. Brigitte K. Goldstein, "Jewish Identification Among the Jews of New Mexico: The Maintenance of Jewishness and Judaism in the Integrated Setting of a Sunbelt City" (PhD diss., University of New Mexico, 1988), 136.

27. See Ellen J. McClain, *Embracing the Stranger: Intermarriage and the Future of the American Jewish Community* (New York: Basic Books, 1995), 13–14.

28. Shinedling, "On the Problem of Intermarriage," American Jewish Archives, Cincinnati, OH, 10.

29. Ibid., 9–10.

30. "Reinventing Our Jewish Community: Can the West Be Won?" December 1994, 31, Jewish Federation of Greater Albuquerque Records (henceforth JFR).

31. Goldstein, "Jewish Identification," 136–37.

32. Ibid., 139.

33. "Mixed Marriages and Mixed Relationships, Temple Beth Shalom," Beth Shalom Archive, November 1988.

34. Sachar, *A History of the Jews in the Modern World*, 695.

Chapter 4

1. See Jack Wertheimer, "Jewish Organizational Life in the United States Since 1945," *AJYB* 95 (1995): 5.

2. *AJYB* 41 (1939–40): 445–518.

3. Ibid., 539.

4. See Tobias, *History*, 147.

5. State Corporation Commission of New Mexico, "Certificate of Incorporation of Albuquerque Jewish Welfare Fund, Inc." February 27, 1948; see also Tobias, *History*, 184–85.

6. See Wertheimer, "Jewish Organizational Life in the United States," 15.

7. The AJWF and its successors contain the financial reports of the organization. In addition, the *Link* published reports of collections and allocations.

8. AJWF, "Schedule of Allocations Paid for the Years 1946, 1947, 1948, 1949, 1950."

9. *Link* 26, no. 5 (May 1997): 1, 10.

10. Ibid.

11. Michael G. Sutin, "A Brief Report Concerning Some People, Events and Issues in the Life of the JCCA," JFR, 3–4.

12. "Minutes of the Executive Directors Conference held on July 14, 15, 16, 1967, Los Angeles, California," JFR, 3.

13. AJWF, Minutes, "President's Annual Report," December 3, 1967, JFR.

14. [M. C. Gettinger], "Evaluation and Recommendations Re: The Jewish Community Council of Albuquerque," [1981], JFR, 3, 8.

15. *Link* 26, no. 5 (May 1997): 10.

16. AJWF, Federation Minutes, June 25, 1970, JFR.

17. *Link* 1, no. 5 (April 1972): 1.

18. Ibid.

19. Interview with Andrew Lipman, Executive Director, Jewish Federation of Greater Albuquerque, 2003.

20. "Chronology of Major Action," JFR, 8.

21. Ibid., 14.

22. *Link* 3, no. 5 (February 1974): 4.

23. *Link* 13, no. 6 (June 1984): 1.

24. "Chronology of Major Action," JFR, n.d., 6.

25. Ibid., January 23, 1975, 21.

26. AJWF, "Allocations," completed November 29, 1960, JFR.

27. *Link* 15, no. 1 (January 1986): 3.

28. *Link* 18, no. 9 (October 1989): 1.

29. *Link* 18, no. 1 (January 1989): 1.

30. "Financial Report: Annual Dinner Meeting," December 3, 1967, JFR.

31. AJWF, "Minutes, President's Annual Report," December 3, 1967, JFR, 1.

32. The figures are derived from tables in the minutes of the AJWF and those published in the *Link*.

33. "Chronology of Major Action," JFR, 7.

34. *Link* 21, no. 9 (October 1992): 1.

35. JCC, Community Needs and Assessment and Space Program, [1993], JFR, 7.

36. Ibid.

37. *Link* 21, no. 6 (June 1992): 2; *Link* 24, no. 1 (January 1995): 1; *Link* 29, no. 10 (November 2000): 10.

38. "Remarks by Rabbi Paul Citrin," February 12, 1993, Israel C. Carmel Archive.

39. Ibid.

40. *Link* 24, no. 6 (June 1995): 1, 7.

41. *Link* 29, no. 11 (December 2000): 3.

42. *Link* 30, no. 11 (December 2001): 1, 15.

43. *Link* 27, no. 1 (January 1998): 1, 8.

44. *Link* 29, no. 10 (November 1998): 7.

45. *Link* 24, no. 8 (September 1995): 1.

46. *Link* 4, no. 8 (May 1975): 1.

47. *Link* 25, no. 11 (December 1996): 1.

48. Ibid., 8.

49. See William J. Parish, *The Charles Ilfeld Company: The Rise and Decline of Mercantile Capitalism in New Mexico* (Cambridge, MA: Harvard University Press, 1961).

50. See Floyd S. Fierman, *Guts and Ruts* (New York: Ktav, 1985); and Floyd S. Fierman, *Roots and Boots* (Hoboken, NJ: Ktav, 1987).

51. A. David Scholder, "In the beginning . . . ," typescript in the possession of the author.

52. *New Mexico Jewish Historical Society* 1, no. 3 (1987): [1].

53. New Mexico Jewish Historical Society, Membership Directory, April 2000.

54. Tomas Jaehn, comp., *Jewish Pioneers of New Mexico* (Santa Fe: Museum of New Mexico Press, 2004), 8.

55. "JSU," *Out of the Desert* 11, no. 1 (Winter 1971–72): [7].

56. "Memoirs of an Attorney," American Jewish Archives, Cincinnati, OH, mss collection no. 112, 99.

57. Minutes, June 25, 1970, AJWF.

58. Rothenberg, "JSU."

59. *Link* 16, no. 8 (October 1987): 19.

60. Federation Minutes, AJWF, June 1993.

61. Ryan Florsheim, "Hillel House Provides Connections," *Daily Lobo*, August 26, 2002, 1.

62. See chapter 7, "Issues," for the specific nature of the matters treated.

63. "ADL Names Nodel President," *Link* 21, no. 8 (September 1992): 9.

64. *Link* 27, no. 4 (April 1998): 8–9. See also chapter 7, "Issues."

65. Peter Hess, "Mazel Tov Santa Fe," *Link* 13, no. 4 (February 1984): 4.

Chapter 5

1. "Directory of Churches and Religious Organizations in New Mexico, 1940" (Albuquerque: The New Mexico Historical Records Survey, 1940), 144–46.

2. See appendix for a listing in the *Link*.

3. Jules B. Grad, *A Time for Dedication: Temple Albert*, September 8 and 9, 1984, 34–35, 38.

4. Ibid., 34.

5. See chapter 6, "Interfaith Activity," and chapter 7, "Issues."

6. Gunther Rothenberg, *Congregation Albert, 1897–1972*, Israel C. Carmel Archive, 35; Congregation Albert, *Membership Directory*, 5671 (2000–2001).

7. Grad, *A Time for Dedication*, 64.

8. *Congregation B'nai Israel Year Book*, 5762 (2001).

9. *Link* 26, no. 8 (September 1997): 1, 13.

10. Sharon Niederman, "A Home At Last," *The Reporter*, Winter 2000, 7.

11. Lynn Gottlieb, *She Who Dwells Within* (San Francisco: HarperOne, 1995), 215–16.

12. See chapter 7, "Issues."

13. Gottlieb, *She Who Dwells Within*, 13.

14. Sarah Blustain, "It Helps to Be a Feminist," *Lilith*, Fall 2000, 11.

15. *Link* 29, no. 6 (June–July 2000): 1, 4.

16. *Link* 22, no. 9 (October 1993): 7.

17. *Link* 2, no. 10 (June 1973): 1–2; interview with Professor Noel Pugach, 2002.

18. Interview with Professor Noel Pugach, 2002; "Introduction to Chavurat Hamidbar Prepared for New and Potential Members," in author's possession.

19. "Hasidism," *Encyclopedia Judaica*, vol. 7 (Jerusalem: Keter Pub., 1971), 1390–391.

20. *Link* 21, no. 11 (December 1992): 1–2.

21. James F. Meline, *Two Thousand Miles on Horseback: Santa Fe and Back* (Albuquerque, NM: Horn and Wallace, 1966), 192.

22. Albert Rosenfeld, "In Santa Fe, the City Different: Old Settlers and New," *Commentary* 17, no. 5 (May 1954): 456.

23. "Old Minutes of the Board of Directors," Temple B'nai Israel, Santa Fe.

24. Frances Levine, "Temple Beth Shalom," draft of "The Seventies Scene at TBS," 2, manuscript in author's possession.

25. *Link* 19, no. 8 (September 1990): 20.

26. Secretary, Beit Tikvah, telephone interview, August 2, 2005.

27. "Board Minutes," Temple Beth Shalom, May 6, 1985, 2.

28. L. E. Freudenthal, May 21, 1947, box 12, Freudenthal Family Papers, Rio Grande Historical Collections, New Mexico State University Library.

29. Ibid.

30. Historical account by Mr. and Mrs. Leland S. Trafton, box 12, Freudenthal Family Papers, Rio Grande Historical Collections, New Mexico State University Library.

31. Richard J. Lease, "Eugene J. Stern: Merchant, Farmer and Philanthropist of Las Cruces, New Mexico," *Western States Jewish Historical Quarterly* 9, no. 2 (January 1977): 165.

32. For studies on the early growth of Rio Rancho, see Joseph E. Weiss, "Sunbelt Migration and Its Effects Upon the Growth and Development of a Southwest Community" (PhD diss., University of New Mexico, 1981); Sheila Jane Furstenberg, "Rio Rancho 1961–1982: A History," Rio Rancho Public Library.

33. Weiss, "Sunbelt Migration and Its Effects," 143.

34. Rio Rancho Jewish Center scrapbook, January 30, 1982.

35. Paul Sperling, "Jews of Early Los Alamos," *Western States Jewish History* 18, no. 4 (July 1986): 355.

36. Cited in Karen Hack, "The Formation of a Jewish Community in Los Alamos," research paper, UNM–Los Alamos, 1991, 2.

37. Ibid., 7.

38. *Link* 26, no. 11 (December 1997): 9.

39. *Link* 17, no. 1 (January 1988): 4.

40. Iris Keltz, *Scrapbook of a Taos Hippie* (El Paso, TX: Cinco Puntos Press, 2000); "Searching for a Village: A Wandering Jew in the Counter Culture of Northern New Mexico" (paper given at the New Mexico Jewish Historical Society Annual Conference, Taos, 2002).

41. *Link* 31, no. 5 (May 2002): 1, 7.

42. Ibid.

43. *Link* 28, no. 9 (October 1998): 7.

44. *Link* 27, no. 2 (February 1998): 1.

45. Ibid.

46. Ibid.

47. *Link* 31, no. 8 (September 2002): 4, 6.

48. *Link* 31, no. 7 (August 2002): 1, 14.

49. *Link* 17, no. 3 (March 1988): 3.

50. Ibid.

51. Ibid.

52. James D. Shinkle, *Fifty Years of Roswell History, 1867–1917* (Roswell, NM: Hall-Poorbaugh Press, 1964).

53. "The Jewish Community in Roswell: A Brief History," (Chaves County Historical Museum, Roswell, NM), 4.

54. Estelle Matus to author, December 10, 2006.

55. Undated letter signed by the secretary, Roswell, NM, in author's possession.

56. "Jewish Community in Roswell," 4.

57. Interview with Seymour Beckerman, Roswell, 1986.

58. Telephone interview with Mrs. Carolyn Sidd, May 2, 2005.

59. *Link* 28, no. 6 (June–July 1999): 6–7.

60. Walking Stick Foundation, October 2006, retrieved from walkingstick.org.

61. *Link* 28, no. 6 (June–July 1999): 6–7.

62. *Link* 28, no. 8 (September 1998): 1, 14, 15.

63. "From the Rabbi's Study," *Link* 11, no. 6 (June 1982): 8.

Chapter 6

1. See Tobias, *History of the Jews in New Mexico*, 156.

2. Augustin Cardinal Bea, *The Church and the Jewish People* (New York: Geoffrey Chapman, 1966), 157–58.

3. Michael Glazier and Thomas J. Shelley, eds., *Encyclopedia of American Catholic History* (Collegeville, MN: Liturgical Press, 1997), 110, 170.

4. U.S. Conference of Catholic Bishops, *Reflections on Covenant and Mission*, Washington, DC, August 12, 2002, 3.

5. Anti-Defamation League, "Regional Advisory Board and ADL Friends"; *Denver Catholic Register*, April 13, 1961, 1.

6. Randi Jones Walker, "Protestantism in Modern New Mexico," in *Religion in Modern New Mexico*, ed. Ferenc M. Szasz and Richard W. Etulain (Albuquerque: University of New Mexico Press, 1997), 52.

7. Janice E. Schuetz, "A Rhetorical Approach to Protestant Evangelism in Twentieth Century New Mexico," in Szasz and Etulain, *Religion in Modern New Mexico*, 139.

8. *Albuquerque Tribune*, October 14, 1977, A3.

9. Israel C. Carmel Archive, Congregation Albert Men's Club Minutes, August 16, 1955; October 12, 1955.

10. "Rabbi Shor Sermons," Israel C. Carmel Archive, December 20, 1963, 1.

11. Ibid.

12. Ibid., December 12, 1969.

13. Ibid.

14. Ibid.

15. *Presbyterian Peaks* 8, no. 6 (September–October 1969): 3; *Presbyterian Peaks* 9, no. 6 (October 1970): 2.

16. See *Baptist New Mexican*, September 9, 1972.

17. *Link* 4, no. 7 (April 1975): 7.

18. *Link* 7, no. 4 (April 1978): 1.

19. *Link* 25, no. 6 (June 1996): 1; Rev. Ernest Falardeau, "A Short History of the Jewish-Catholic Dialogue in Albuquerque, New Mexico 1982–1993," 2–3, in possession of author.

20. John Temple, "Catholics, Jews Mark 20 Years of Peace," *Albuquerque Tribune*, October 26, 1985, A5.

21. Falardeau, "A Short History of the Jewish-Catholic Dialogue," 1–2.

22. *Albuquerque Journal North*, February 21, 1997, 5N.

23. Paul Logan, "Sheehan to Speak at Synagogue," *Albuquerque Journal*, June 23, 2000, D2; Jan Jonas, "Archbishop's Historic Speech Aims at Jewish Reconciliation," *Albuquerque Tribune*, June 22, 2000, 1A.

24. *Link* 25, no. 3 (March 1996): 2, 12; telephone interview with Susan Sandager, February 4, 2003; *Yad B'Yad*, September 1998.

25. *Yad B'Yad*, September 1998.

26. *Link* 23, no. 6 (June 1994): 1, 11.

27. *Link* 25, no. 7 (1996): 1, 5.

28. *Link* 25, no. 3 (March 1996): 2.

29. *Yad B'Yad*, March 2000.

30. See chapter 7, "Issues," on this theme.

31. *Link* 18, no. 3 (March 1989): 11.

32. *Link* 24, no. 4 (April 1995): 12.

Chapter 7

1. David Boroff, "A New Yorker's Report of New Mexico," *Harper's Magazine* 230, no. 1377 (February 1965): 72.

2. Tobias, *History*, 192–94.

3. "Milton Seligman (MS) Interview," Peter Tannen, interviewer, July 17, 1997, 8, Congregation Albert Oral History Project.

4. Tobias, *History*, 193.

5. Ibid., 191.

6. David Caplovitz and Candace Rogers, *Swastika 1960: The Epidemic of Anti-Semitic Vandalism in America* (New York: Anti-Defamation League of B'nai B'rith, 1961), 22, 24.

7. *Link* 11, no. 9 (October 1982): 5.

8. *Link* 23, no. 5 (May 1994): 1, 4.

9. *Link* 17, no. 7 (July 1988): 6.

10. *Link* 4, no. 3 (December 1974): 7.

11. Wertheimer, "Jewish Organizational Life," 10–12.

12. Ibid.

13. Ibid.

14. Rabbi David Shor, "Sermons," Israel C. Carmel Archive, March 27, 1958.

15. "Minutes," Jewish Welfare Fund, July 27, 1967.

16. Paul Sperling, "Jews of Early Los Alamos: A Memoir," *Western States Jewish History* 18, no. 4 (July 1986): 358–60.

17. *RCAR Fact Sheet* (Washington, DC: Religious Coalition for Abortion Rights, n.d.).

18. "Chronology of Major Action," December, 15, 1977, 24.

19. Ibid., June 22, 1978, 24.

20. *Link* 18, no. 10 (November 1989): 1.

21. *Albuquerque Tribune*, October 14, 1989, A7.
22. *Link* 18, no. 10 (November 1989): 1.
23. Janice E. Scheutz, "A Rhetorical Approach to Protestant Evangelism in Twentieth-Century New Mexico," in Szasz and Etulain, *Religion in Modern New Mexico*, 136–38.
24. *AJYB* 51 (1950): 98–99.
25. "The Seligman Family," *Jewish Pioneers of New Mexico* (Albuquerque: New Mexico Jewish Historical Society, 2005), 14.
26. Rabbi David Shor, early undated sermon, Israel C. Carmel Archive.
27. *Link* 6, no. 7 (July–August 1977): 1.
28. Congregation Albert Bulletin, March 1985, 8.
29. Congregation Albert Bulletin, January 1987.
30. *Link* 14, no. 12 (December 1985): 3.
31. *Link* 17, no. 4 (April 1988): 1.
32. *Link* 18, no. 11 (December 1989): 10–11.
33. *Link* 23, no. 5 (May 1994): 5.
34. *Link* 27, no. 3 (March 1998): 1, 12.
35. Rabbi David Shor, "Sermons," n.d., Israel C. Carmel Archive.
36. *Link* 26, no. 3 (March 1997): 1.
37. Interview with Pauline Eisenstadt, 2007.
38. See Tobias, *History*, 7–21. For a full description of the crypto-Jews see Stanley M. Hordes, *To the End of the Earth* (New York: Columbia University Press, 2005).
39. See Bernard Postal and Leonard Koppman, *Jewish Tourist's Guide* (Philadelphia: Jewish Publication Society of America, 1954), 330.
40. See Tobias, *History*, 20–21.
41. Copy of letter in author's possession.
42. Hordes, *To the End of the Earth*. The volume includes Hordes's research findings conducted over a twenty-five-year period.
43. Ibid., 234–36.
44. Ibid., xvi.
45. Interview with Rabbi Lynn Gottlieb.

46. *Albuquerque Tribune*, "Jewish Traditions," November 22, 1990, C1.

47. Paul J. Citrin, introduction to "Modern Descendants of Conversos in New Mexico" by David S. Nidel, *Western States Jewish History* 16, no. 3 (April 1984): 249–51.

48. See for example "El Grito," *La Herencia del Norte* 24 (Winter 1999): 7.

49. *Link* 26, no. 11 (December 1997): 1, 13; *Albuquerque Journal*, March 2, 1997, 1D.

50. David Steinberg, "Holocaust Sculpture Splits Jewish Community," *Albuquerque Journal*, September 24, 1997, 1A.

51. *Link* 26, no. 6 (June 1997): 1.

Chapter 8

1. "Out West," 1904. Reprinted in *El Palacio* 18, nos. 10–11 (June 1, 1925): 223–29.

2. Edna Robertson and Sarah Nestor, *Artists of the Canyons and Caminos: Santa Fe, the Early Years* (Santa Fe, NM: n.p., 1976), 11.

3. Bart Ripp, *Albuquerque Tribune*, November 23, 1987, B1.

4. Mabel Dodge Luhan, *Movers and Shakers* (New York: Harcourt and Brace, 1936), 534–35.

5. Sharon Niederman, "Jewish Artists Contribute to State's Cultural Mosaic," *New Mexico Magazine* 72, no. 12 (December 1994): 34–43.

6. Judy Chicago, *Beyond the Flower: The Autobiography of a Feminist Artist* (New York: Viking, 1996), 173.

7. *Link* 32, no. 4 (April 2003): 14.

8. *Link* 25, no. 9 (October 1996): 10.

9. *Link* 24, no. 4 (April 1995): 7.

10. *Link* 14, no. 10 (October 1985): 4.

11. John Atkinson, "The Day the Music Died," *Stereophile*, March 2005.

12. Congregation B'nai Israel, "Congregation B'nai Israel," n.d. (1960?).

13. David Boroff, "A New Yorker's Report on New Mexico," 72.

14. Congregation Albert Oral History Project, "Milton Seligman Interview—March 5, 1997," 18.

15. Jerry Palmer, "A Brief Guide to Ethnic Eating in New Mexico," *Link* 16, no. 2 (February 1987): 2.

16. Ibid.

17. *Link* 22, no. 1 (January 1993): 1.

18. *Link* 27, no. 1 (January 1998): 4.

19. *Albuquerque Journal*, January 16, 1992, D3.

20. *Link* 19, no. 9 (October 1990): 14.

21. *Albuquerque Journal*, October 25, 1992, B1.

22. *Albuquerque Tribune*, March 13, 1992, A6.

23. *Link* 26, no. 9 (October 1997): 1, 9.

24. Ibid.

25. *Link* 29, no. 8 (September 2000): 14.

26. Ibid.

27. *Albuquerque Journal*, October 14, 1959, A1, A15.

28. Wesley Pulkka, "Architect/Artist Built National Reputation," *Albuquerque Journal*, July 27, 2003, F5.

29. *Albuquerque Journal*, January 25, 1990, 9C; telephone interview, Helen Grevey, June 20, 2005.

30. Interview with Robert Nordhaus, April 15, 2000.

31. See also chapter 6, "Interfaith Activity."

Index

Page numbers in italics indicate illustrations.

abortion, 111–13
Abruzzo, Ben, 141
Acoma Pueblo, 103
Adler, Rana, 41–42
AJWF. *See* Albuquerque Jewish Welfare Fund (AJWF)
Alamogordo, New Mex., 86
Albert, Harold, 41
Albuquerque Jewish Welfare Fund (AJWF): and civil rights, 111; creation of, 38–39; as Jewish Community Council of Albuquerque (JCCA), 43–45, 112; as Jewish Federation of Greater Albuquerque (JFGA), 45, 53, 56, 115–16, 122–24
Albuquerque, New Mex.: congregations, 1–2, 62–73, 147; interfaith activity, 97–100; population growth, 10–11; social and economic change, 22–24. *See also* Congregation

Albert; Congregation B'nai Israel
Amar, Paula, 57
American Furniture, 140
American Indians, 83, 88, 102–4, 141
American Jewish Committee (AJC), 112
American Jewish Year Book (AJYB), 8, 149n3
American Nazi Party, 107
American Realty and Petroleum Corporation (Amrep), 80
Anti-Defamation League (ADL) of B'nai B'rith: and anti-Semitism, 107–10; and civil rights, 57–58; Jewish-Catholic Dialogue, 100; and Santa Ana Pueblo, 103; on separation of church and state, 116–17
anti-Semitism: and abortion, 112–13; and ADL, 107–10; and the Catholic Church, 94–95, 100; evangelizing Jews, 101–2; Holocaust memorial (Albuquerque), 122–24;

Holocaust Remembrance days, 98; and the Lebanese-Israeli war, 58; and Polisar, 138; prewar, 93–94, 106

Anusim Yisrael (The Forced Ones of Israel), 122

Archdiocese of Santa Fe, 15, 96, 98, 100

artists, 127–31

Ashkenazic population, 98, 119, 120, 122

assimilation, 3–4, 24–26

bagels, 134

Barry, Anna, 128

Beckerman, Seymour, 87

Bibo, Solomon, 103

Bittner, Beatrice, 47

Black, Rabbi Joseph R., 65, 118

Blaugrund, Emanual, 140

Blaugrund, Ilse, 51

B'nai B'rith (Sons of the Covenant): creation of, 1, 74; and the Hillel group, 56; and the Jewish Community Council, 58; Lodge, 82; prewar, 37

B'nai Shalom, 83

Brotherhood Days, 93

Bruns Army General Hospital, 74

Cafe Europa, 58

Cahn, Mrs. Stuart, 30

Carlsbad, New Mex., 15–16, 85–86, 148

Carr, Judith, 54

Catholic Church, 25, 94–95, 100, 113–18

Celnik, Rabbi Isaac, 67–69, 99, 109, 117, 121

Chabad (House of Worship), 73, 78

Chávez, Fray Angélico, 119

Chavez, Mayor Martin, 124

chavurah, 71, 78, 83, 86

Chavurat Hamidbar (Fellowship of the Desert), 71–73

Chicago, Judy, 130

Christian Heritage Week, 116

Citrin, Rabbi Paul, 65; on abortion, 112–13; on crypto-Judaism, 121; his career, 63–64; Jewish-Catholic Dialogue, 98, 100; and the Jewish Community Center, 49–50; on religion in public schools, 115

civil rights, 57–58, 107, 111–13

Cohen, Abe and Sophia, 49

Cold War, 107

Congregation Albert: and abortion, 112; and anti-Semitism, 109; creation of, 1, 61; its stability and growth, 62–65; and the Jewish Community Center, 49–50; membership, 22; and women, 30–32

Congregation Beit Tikva, 78

Congregation B'nai Israel: and anti-Semitism, 109; and Archbishop Sheehan, 100; creation of, 1–2, 61; its growth, 67–69; and kosher foods, 132; location, 63; membership, 21–22, 27–28; and women, 30–32; and the Zionist Organization of America, 38

Congregation Montefiore, 1, 61

Congregation Nahalat Shalom (Inheritance of Peace), 69–70, 121

crypto-Judaism, 83, 84, 118–22

Cuba, New Mex., 88, 148

culture: and assimilation, 3–4, 24–26; and communication, 53–54; and community, 48–51; and expressing Jewishness, 98, 144

Dave's Kosher Meats, 133
Domenici, Sen. Pete, 110
Duke City Lumber Company, 140
Duran, Dennis, 121–22

economy: and the arts, 127–31; and entrepreneurs, 21–24, 28–29, 138–41; prewar, 4; service sector, 27
ecumenical councils, 96
education: and allocations, 45–46; GI Bill, 19–20; Hebrew schools, 49, 72, 76, 78–79, 81–83; and Jewish history, 141–42; in Las Vegas, 85; and occupations, 21–24; PhDs, 18, 19; prewar, 4; public schools, 113–18; and women, 29–32
Efroymson, Miriam, 41
Eisenstadt, Sen. Pauline, 118, 136, 137
entrepreneurs, 21–24, 28–29, 138–41
ethnic character, 1, 3–4
evolution, 117, 118
Experiment in Jewish Learning, 44
Experiment in Jewish Living, 69

Falardeau, Rev. Ernest, 98, 113
Federation of Jewish Charities, 38
Feldman, Rabbi John, 56
Fierman, Rabbi Floyd, 54
Fine, Art, 47
Flatow, Max, 139–40

Fleischer, Max N., 65
foods, 132–34
Fred Harvey's News and Curio Department, 127
Freudenthal, L. E., 79

Gaines, Janet, 56
Gans, Julius, 74, 127
Gardenswartz, Judy and Arthur, 41, 49
Gardenswartz, Shirley, 52
Gellert, Werner, 58
Getty, Rita, 117
GI Bill, 19–20
Goldberg, Rabbi Shlomo, 79
Gold, Jake, 127
Gonzales, Belarmino R. "Blackie," 101
Gottlieb, Rabbi Lynn, 69–70, 71, 115, 130, 138
Greenberg, Milton, 133
Grevey, Joe and Jack, 140
Groves, Gen. Leslie, 19
Gusowsky, Florence, 49

Hadassah chapter, 51–52, 58, 82, 100–101
Harry and Jeanette Weinberg Foundation, 49
Harvie, Keith, 41
Hasidism, 73
Helman, Rabbi Leonard, 76–78, 90–91
Hertzmark, Marcia, 74
Herz, Cary, 131
Hillel Foundation, 39
Hillel group, 56–57
Hobbs, New Mex., 86

Hoffman, Sam, 139
Hoffmantown Church, 51
Holocaust memorial
  (Albuquerque), 122–24
Holocaust Remembrance days, 98
Home for the Jewish Aged project,
  44–45
Hordes, Dr. Stanley M., 119, 120

Ilfeld Company, 84, 140–41
Ilfeld family, 2, 139
immigration: after World War
  II, 21; aid for families, 47;
  Ashkenazic population, 98,
  119, 120, 122; in the East, 24–26;
  and ethnic character, 1, 3–4;
  prewar, 1, 3, 125–27
Intel, 20
interfaith activity, 51, 94–104
Interfaith Thanksgiving services,
  98
Israel: anti-Israel views, 107;
  and anti-Semitism, 58; and
  Congressional representatives, 110, 136; and Evangelical
  Christians, 100–101; funds for,
  47–48, 59; immigrants, 20; and
  Rabbi Gottlieb, 70; support for,
  39, 45, 110–11
Israel Day celebration, 44

JCCA. See Jewish Community
  Council of Albuquerque
  (JCCA)
Jewish Braille Institute, 39
Jewish-Catholic Dialogue, 98, 100
Jewish Community Center, 48–51
Jewish Community Council of
  Albuquerque (JCCA): and
  abortion, 112; as Albuquerque
  Jewish Welfare Fund (AJWF),
38–39, 43, 44, 111; as Jewish
  Federation of Greater
  Albuquerque (JFGA), 45, 53,
  56, 115–16, 122–24; raising
  funds, 43–45
Jewish Community Council of
  Santa Fe, 58–59
Jewish Family Service, 47, 48, 49
Jewish Federation of Greater
  Albuquerque (JFGA): as
  Albuquerque Jewish Welfare
  Fund (AJWF), 38–39, 43, 44,
  111; and the Hillel group, 56;
  and the Holocaust Memorial,
  122–24; as Jewish Community
  Council of Albuquerque
  (JCCA), 43–45, 112; and the
  Link, 53; and organizational
  expansion, 45; on religion in
  public schools, 115–16
Jewish Renewal, 83
Jewish Theological Seminary, 39
JFGA. See Jewish Federation of
  Greater Albuquerque (JFGA)
Jicarilla Apaches, 141
Joint Defense Appeal, 45
Judaic Institute for Christian
  Clergy, 97–98

kabbalah, 90
Karni, Michaela, 102
Karni, Prof. Shlomo, 52, 53
Kehillat Torah HaMidbar, 78
Kellogg, Leah, 75
Keltz, Iris, 83
Klein, Rabbi Yisroel, 34
Kubie, Kurt, 40

LaBorwit, Melanie, 84
Ladino, 121
language, 3, 121
Las Cruces, New Mex., 13, 52,
    79–80, 108, 148
Las Vegas Montefiore Cemetery
    Committee, 84
Las Vegas, New Mex.: congrega-
    tions, 1, 61, 84–85, 147; formal
    organizations, 1; and the New
    Mexico Jewish Historical
    Society, 55, 84; population
    growth, 15; and the railroad, 3
Lehman, Daniel, 87
Liberman, Maurice, 140
Lieberman, Sen. Joseph, 138
Link, 16, 53–54, 85, 131, 134
Lipman, Andrew, 44, 51
Londer, Shirlee, 41
Los Alamos, New Mex.: congrega-
    tions, 81–82, 148; creation of,
    18–19; Hadassah chapter, 52;
    population growth, 13–14; and
    Santa Fe, 74
Lovato, Jake, 123, 124
Luhan, Mabel Dodge, 128

Magidson's restaurant, 132–33
Manhattan Project, 14
Markovitz, Rabbi Sam, 76–78
marriage, 30–34, 103
Medoff, Mark, 131
Meem, John Gaw, 76
Merrian, Mark, 85
Meyer, Leopold, 38
mezuzahs, 84
Midbar Co-op, 134
mikvah, 73

Ministerial Alliance of Santa Fe,
    100
Mishkan Shalom, 86
Montana, Roy, 103
Moskowitz, Ira, 128
musicians, 131–32

National Conference of Christian
    Bishops, 95
National Conference of Christians
    and Jews, 93
Native American–Jewish
    Dialogue, 103
Navajos, 88, 103
Nazism, 58, 107
New Buffalo, 83
New Hope Church, 51
Newman Center for Catholic
    Students, 15
New Mexico Council of Churches,
    96, 100, 115
New Mexico Holocaust and
    Intolerance Museum, 58
New Mexico Jewish Historical
    Society, 54–55, 84
New Mexico Jewish Link, 54. See
    also *Link*
New Mexico Magazine, 126–27
New Mexico State University, 108
New Mexico Symphony Orchestra,
    131
New York, New York, 24–26
Nodel, Richard, 58
Nordhaus, Max, 141
Nordhaus, Robert, 141
Nostra Aetate (In Our Time), 94
Novenson, Sara, 130–31

Oppenheimer, J. Robert, 19
organizations: formal, 2, 26; religious, 89–90; secular, 36–38, 42–48. *See also* individual organizations
Orthodox Judaism, 61, 78, 79, 112

Pardes Yisroel, 78
Parish, William J., 54
Pick, Marcel and Emil, 74
Picraux, Denise, 117
Plaut, Florence, 87
Polisar, Joseph, 136, 138
politics, 113–18, 134–38
Pope John XXIII, 94
population: after World War II, 7–10; in Albuquerque, 10–11; in Carlsbad, 15; counting religious groups, 7–8; in Las Cruces, 13; in Las Vegas, 15; in Los Alamos, 13–14; and retirees, 27–28; in Rio Rancho, 14–15; in Santa Fe, 11–12; in Taos, 16; and urbanization, 17
Protestant groups, 95–96, 115
Pueblo Indians, 83, 102–4
Pugach, Prof. Noel, 141

railroads, 2, 138–39
Reconstructionism, 86
Reform Judaism, 78, 86, 112
Reinman, Marilyn, 30
religion: in 2000, 61–62; in Albuquerque, 62–73; and the Catholic Church, 25; and censuses, 7–8; crypto-Judaism, 83, 84, 118–22; ecumenical movement, 97–100; evangelizing Jews, 101–2; Hasidism, 73; and health services, 27;

Hebrew schools, 49, 72, 76, 78–79, 81–83; interfaith activity, 94–104; Orthodoxy, 61, 78, 79, 112; Protestant groups, 95–96; in public schools, 113–18; Reconstructionism, 86; Reform Judaism, 78, 86, 112; and religious expression, 69–73, 78–79, 82–83, 86–90, 144; and secular organizations, 49–51, 89–90. *See also* individual organizations
Religious Coalition for Abortion Rights (RCAR), 112
retirees, 27–28, 69, 80
Rio Rancho, New Mex., 14–15, 20, 52, 80–81
Rockwell, George Lincoln, 107
Roswell, New Mex., 86–88, 147
Rothenberg, Prof. Gunther, 56, 141
Roth, Henry, 131
Rubenstein, Louis, 76
Ruidoso, New Mex., 86
Rusk, Mayor David, 122

Sandager, John, 51
Sandager, Susan, 102
Sandia Corporation, 19
Sanford, Mark, 85
Santa Ana Pueblo, 103
Santa Fe Jewish Temple, 74
Santa Fe Jewish Temple and Community Center, Inc., 76
Santa Fe, New Mex.: B'nai B'rith, 74, 82; congregations, 74–79, 147; formal organizations, 2, 12; Hadassah chapter, 52; interfaith activity, 100, 101; Jewish Community Council, 58–59; and kosher foods, 133–34; and the New Mexico

Jewish Historical Society, 55; population growth, 11–12; and the railroad, 2–3; social and economic change, 28–29; and women, 30–32
Schiff, Steve, *135*, 136
Schlachter, Jack, 82
Schmuckler, Rabbi Chaim, 73, 117, 133, 138
Scholder, A. David, 54
school prayer, 115
Schultz, Paul, 133
Schwartz, Mel, 57
Schweitzer, Herman, 127
Seligman, Arthur, 134
Seligman, Dr. Randolph, 141
Seligman family, 2, 65, 114
Seligman, Milton, 40, 57, 107, 133, 136
Seligman, Susan, 57–58, 109
Sephardic Messianic congregations, 121
shamanism, 88
Sheehan, Archbishop Michael J., *99*, 100
Shinedling, Rabbi Abraham, 33, 76
Shor, Rabbi David, 33–34, 56, 63, 96–97, 114, 117
Simon, Elisa, 47
Solomon Schechter Day School, 49
Sons of the Covenant. *See* B'nai B'rith
Southern Baptist Conventions, 101
Southwest Arts and Crafts Company, 127
Spanish Inquisition, 118
Specter, David, 45
Spiegelberg, Abe, 127
Spiegelberg family, 2, 55

Staab family, 2
Sterne, Maurice, 128
Stolaroff, Sam, 87
Straser, Aron, 81
Stulberg, Neal, 131–32
Sussman, Arthur, 128, *129*
Sutin family, 40
Sutin, Jonathan, 110
Sutin, Lewis, *40*, 56
Sutin, Michael, *41*, 43, 44, 57
Swastika, 108
Synagogue Council of America, 46
Szilard, Leo, 19

Taichert, Daniel, 74
Taichert, Milton, 84
Taos Minyan, 83
Taos, New Mex., 16, 52, 82–83, 148
Teller, Edward, 19
Temple Albert Men's Club (TAMC), 97
Temple Beth-El, 80
Temple Beth Shalom, 12, 30–32, 58, 74–76, 100
Temple B'nai Israel, 87
Tijerina, Reies, 107–8
tourism, 11
Tucker, Richard, 87

United Jewish Appeal (UJA), 38, 45, 58, 101
University of New Mexico, 19–20, 56–57
urbanization, 17

Vatican II, 94, 95

Walking Stick Foundation, 88, 103
Warburg, Felix and Susan, 55
Ward, Rabbi Nahum, 78
Waste Isolation Pilot Plant
    (WIPP), 85
Weinstein, Yale, 40, 44
Weizman Institute of Science, 39
Wertheim, Joseph and Herman, 85
Winkler, Rabbi Gershon, 88–89,
    103
Wishner, Jane, 116
Wolfe's Bagels, 133
women: artists, 130–31; and
    Chavurat Hamidbar, 72; in
    Los Alamos, 82; and marriage,
    31–34; mikvah, 73; in politics,
136; Rabbi Gottlieb, 69–70, 71,
    115, 130, 138; and the women's
    movement, 29–32
World Exhibit (1995), 58
World War II, 5–6
writers, 131

Yad B'Yad, 51, 101, 102
Yeshiva University, 39
Yiddish, 3
Yiddish Scientific Institute
    (YIVO), 46

Zionist Organization of America,
    38

Printed in the USA
CPSIA information can be obtained
at www.ICGtesting.com
CBHW020228210524
8864CB00002B/97